Easy Beaded Knits

Easy Beaded Knits

FUN AND FASHIONABLE
EMBELLISHED DESIGNS
FOR THE NOVICE KNITTER

Jeanette Trotman

kp books
An imprint of F+W Publications, Inc.
888-457-2873

A QUARTO BOOK

Published in North America in 2006
by Krause Publications
700 East State Street
Iola, WI 54990-0001

Library of Congress Number:
2006927365

13-digit ISBN: 978-0-89689-376-4

10-digit ISBN: 0-89689-376-6

Conceived, designed, and produced by
Quarto Publishing plc
The Old Brewery
6 Blundell Street
London N7 9BH

QUA: EBK

EDITOR: Michelle Pickering
ART EDITOR AND DESIGNER: Sheila Volpe
FASHION PHOTOGRAPHY: Andrew Atkinson
MODELS: Kryssy Martin, Irena Tyshyna
GENERAL PHOTOGRAPHY: Martin Norris
ILLUSTRATOR: Kuo Kang Chen
PATTERN CHECKER: Eva Yates
ASSISTANT ART DIRECTOR: Penny Cobb

ART DIRECTOR: Moira Clinch
PUBLISHER: Paul Carslake

Color separation by
Provision Pte Ltd, Singapore
Printed by SNP Leefung
Printers Ltd, China

contents

Quick & easy projects 40

Introduction

WHERE KNITTERS WERE ONCE limited to scratchy wools and garishly colored acrylics, developments in the textile industry have meant that the range of yarns and colors now available to hand knitters is vast and there is something to suit everyone's taste. In addition, the variety of patterns now available, from scarves and garments to bags and jewelry, are tempting both new and lapsed knitters to enjoy the craft.

Beads and sequins can be combined with knitting to create handmade garments and accessories in a range of styles, from sophisticated haute couture to funky streetwear. All you need to learn are the basics of knit, purl, and how to slip a stitch, and then you can combine beads and sequins into your designs. Use frosted beads that match the color of the yarn at cast-on edges for a subtle look, or sprinkle shiny beads in contrasting colors all over the piece to make a more dramatic statement.

The projects in this book cover a range of skill levels so that both novice and experienced knitters can enjoy working with beads and sequins. From the simple jeweled scented sachets (project 19) to the more complex sumptuously soft shrug (project 12), these projects show that knitting is only made better when you add a bit of sparkle!

Where to start

All of the projects in this book are quick and easy to make, but you will find that some are quicker and easier than others. Each knitter learns at a different pace, so what is easy for one person may not be easy for another. If you have been knitting for a few years, you should be able to tackle any of the projects. If you are completely new to knitting, start with the simpler projects and work your way up to the more complex ones as you gain confidence. The smaller accessories are great things for the novice knitter to make because they allow you to experiment with new skills and yarns on an easy-to-manage scale. The projects in this book can be categorized into three levels:

LEVEL 1

Easy, straightforward projects, without much shaping or complicated stitch work, and no color changing. These are ideal for the novice knitter.

Project 1 Funky felted belt, page 42
Project 4 Beaded float choker and bracelet, page 54
Project 6 Buckled satchel, page 59
Project 8 Sequined flapper bag, page 66
Project 10 Dotty denim bag, page 72
Project 13 Sequined collar cape, page 86
Project 15 Luxurious beaded wrap, page 94
Project 19 Jeweled scented sachets, page 108

LEVEL 2

These are not complicated but they do have a bit more shaping, color changing, and detailed stitch work. They are suitable for the average knitter.

Project 2 Slanted sequined scarf, page 46
Project 3 Laced bikini, page 49
Project 5 Snuggly collar and cuffs, page 56
Project 7 Slouchy summer bag, page 62
Project 9 Felted bag and change purse, page 68
Project 11 Beaded float skirt, page 76
Project 18 Floral summer throw, page 104
Project 20 Circular suede pillow, page 111

LEVEL 3

These projects are a bit more challenging, involving more complex stitch work, shaping, and color changing. Try these once you are confident at the previous two levels.

Project 12 Sumptuously soft shrug, page 81
Project 14 Lacy hip-tie v-neck, page 90
Project 16 Optic-striped pillow, page 98
Project 17 Floral striped bolster, page 101

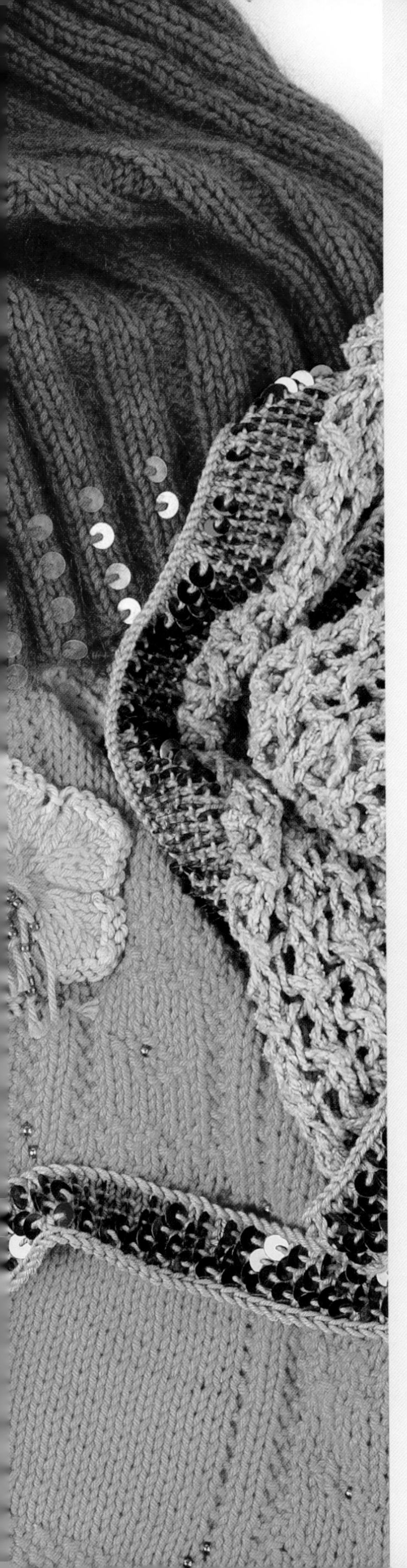

Materials, tools & techniques

This chapter gives guidance on all the materials and tools used to make the projects. If you are new to knitting, read this chapter first and practice the basic techniques of casting on, knitting, purling, and binding off. Then choose a project, and refer to this chapter to learn any additional techniques required. If you already know how to knit, use this chapter to refresh your skills whenever you need to.

Yarn and other materials

The main material used to make the projects in this book is yarn. Although the specific yarns used are listed on pages 124–125, you may wish to knit a project using a different yarn. Understanding the qualities of the types of yarn available will help you choose one that is suitable.

Yarn

Yarn is made by spinning fibers of natural and/or synthetic material together. The combination of fibers used produces yarns of different softness and strength, which affects the look and feel of the finished item as well as what the yarn is like to knit with. Yarn fibers can be split into two categories: natural and synthetic. Some yarns are a blend of natural and synthetic fibers.

Natural fibers

Natural fibers are obtained from either animal or plant origin. Traditionally, wool has been the most popular yarn for hand knitting because of its ability to keep out the cold and wet. Advances in textile technology have made it possible to apply a shrink-resist treatment to wool yarn, making it machine washable. Untreated wool shrinks or "felts" when machine washed, and this can be used to advantage because the fabric produced is durable and can be cut without unraveling. Alpaca and angora fibers tend to be long and create a fluffy fabric with a very soft feel when knitted. Cashmere and silk are beautifully soft but are comparatively expensive because they are regarded as luxury yarns.

Natural fibers of plant origin include cotton, linen, hemp, and ramie/jute. These do not have the same natural elasticity as wool but are ideal for warmer temperatures because they are cool to wear. Cotton is available either combed or with a mercerized coating that gives the yarn a luster that makes it particularly good for showing up stitch detail. When knitted, either type washes well and is cool to wear.

VISCOSE/POLYESTER BLEND

Synthetic yarns

These include rayon, acrylic, polyester, lycra, and nylon. Synthetic yarns are often machine washable and tend to be cheaper than yarns made from natural fibers because they cost less to manufacture. Viscose rayon is actually manufactured from wood pulp and yarns have also been developed in recent years from recycled plastic bottles, textiles, milk, and bamboo.

Yarn blends

Developments in textile technology have meant that it is possible to create yarns that blend two or more fibers together. The resulting blend will have the characteristics if each fiber within the one yarn. Cashmere blends, such as the one used for the luxurious beaded wrap (project 15), combine merino wool, microfiber, and cashmere, giving the finished project the warmth of wool and the softness of cashmere but at a fraction of the cost, while the synthetic element strengthens the yarn. Synthetic yarns are sometimes blended with plant fibers to make them more elastic and help them retain their shape when knitted.

Specialty yarns

Specialty yarns are available to produce particular effects, such as denim-effect cotton, which is designed to shrink and fade like jeans.

Yarn weights

Each strand of fiber used to make yarn is called a ply, and different types of yarn are made from different numbers of plies. The type of fiber, number of plies, and method of spinning all affect the thickness and weight of the finished yarn. Traditionally, there were standard thicknesses of yarn, such as sport and bulky, but nowadays there are so many different blends and fancy yarns available that these terms may be used for different weights of yarn from one yarn spinner to another. The best thing to do if you are unsure of the weight is to check the ball band to see what size needle to use (see page 14).

The weights of yarn used in this book are:

Light Very fine yarn usually knitted on size 1–3 (2.25–3.25 mm) needles.

Sport About one-and-a-half times the thickness of light-weight yarn, usually knitted on size 3–5 (3.25–3.75 mm) needles.

DK (double knitting) Just under twice the thickness of light-weight yarn, usually knitted on size 5–7 (3.75–4.5 mm) needles.

Aran Just under twice the thickness of DK yarn, usually knitted on size 7–9 (4.5–5.5 mm) needles.

Bulky This can be anything thicker than Aran and may be knitted on size 10 (6 mm) needles upward.

COTTON/MICROFIBER BLEND

MERINO WOOL/ MICROFIBER/CASHMERE BLEND

SPECIALTY DENIM-EFFECT COTTON

Ball bands

Whether it comes in ball or hank form, the yarn you buy will have a band around it that lists a lot of useful information.

1 Company brand and yarn name.
2 Weight and length—This gives the weight of the ball in ounces or grams and length of the yarn in yards or meters. This information is useful for calculating the total length needed to complete a project. You can then compare alternative yarns to see whether more or fewer balls are needed to match the required length.
3 Fiber content.
4 Shade number and dye lot—The shade number is the manufacturer's reference to a particular color; the dye lot number refers to a specific batch of yarn dyed in that color at the same time. The lot number will change from batch to batch. When knitting a project, it is important to buy sufficient yarn from the same dye lot because these can vary slightly in color. If you are not certain how many balls you will need, it is always best to buy one extra. Where possible, keep ball bands or make a note of dye lots for reference.
5 Needle size—This gives a generally recommended needle size to use. The pattern instructions for your project will tell you which specific size to use. Sometimes a pattern will specify a different needle size from that recommended on the ball band in order to achieve a certain look.
6 Gauge—This is the standard number of stitches and rows measured over 4" (10 cm) using the recommended needle size and stockinette stitch. However, check the pattern because the designer may have something else in mind.
7 Washing instructions—These tell you how to wash and take care of the yarn once knitted.

TIP: CHOOSING A DIFFERENT YARN

If you cannot find the specific yarn used in a project, or you would simply prefer to use a different yarn, look at the recommended needle size and gauge provided on the ball band of the yarn that was used in this book (see pages 124–125). Choose a substitute yarn that matches these as closely as possible, but be aware that the number of balls required may be different. Calculate the total length of yarn needed to complete the project by multiplying the number of balls by the length of yarn per ball (you will find this information at the beginning of each project). Then divide the total length of yarn required by the length per ball of the substitute yarn. This will give the number of substitute balls required.

Wire and suede thong

You can knit with materials other than yarn. The sequined flapper bag (project 8) is knitted using enameled copper wire together with cotton yarn, while the front of the circular suede pillow (project 20) is knitted with suede thong.

Other materials

Apart from knitting materials, beads, and sequins, the only other materials used in the projects in this book are:

- Rectangular horn buckle to finish the funky felted belt (project 1), and circular tortoiseshell buckle to fasten the buckled satchel (project 6)
- Ribbon for backing the beaded float choker and bracelet (project 4)
- Zipper for the slouchy summer bag (project 7) and the felted change purse (project 9)
- Sheer ribbon to use as handles and a drawstring on the sequined flapper bag (project 8), and to fasten the sequined collar cape (project 13)
- Lining fabric and pin clip for the dotty denim bag (project 10)
- Denim fabric to make pockets for the beaded float skirt (project 11)
- Square pillow form and shell buttons for the optic-striped pillow (project 16)
- Bolster pillow form for the floral striped bolster (project 17)
- Sheer fabric and dried lavender for the jeweled scented sachets (project 19)
- Furnishing fabric and circular pillow form for the circular suede pillow (project 20), plus rayon cord for sewing on the large beads

All of these items can be purchased from good fabric stores.

Beads and sequins

Central to every project in this book is the use of beads and sequins, which add a glamorous touch to knitted garments and are great for embellishing accessories. Whether worked into the fabric during knitting or sewn on afterward, they can be used to create a range of effects—use them sparingly to create a subtle look, or liberally for a more dramatic effect.

Beads

Beads are made from a variety of materials, including plastic, bone, and wood, but the majority of the projects in this book use glass beads because of the richness of color they create.

When choosing beads, check whether or not they are machine washable. Also make sure that they are the correct size for the yarn you are using. For example, do not use large glass beads with a sport-weight yarn because they will cause the knitting to sag; similarly, avoid using very small beads with bulky-weight yarn because the beading will not stand out enough and the beads may slip through the stitches to the wrong side of the fabric, especially if it is not knitted very tightly.

Always make sure that the hole in the center of the bead is big enough to pass a doubled end of yarn through. When knitting with two ends of yarn at the same time, thread the beads onto the finer yarn, hold the ends of both yarns together, and work as normal.

Seed beads

These small, round glass beads are ideal for embellishing knitted fabrics. They can be sewn onto the finished item, but are also very easy to incorporate into the fabric during knitting. Seed beads are available in a wide variety of sizes and in many different finishes. Some are made with colored glass, while others are transparent and lined with color, which means that the central hole has been painted with color. Seed beads are commonly sold by gram weight.

TIP: BUYING BEADS

Even if a pattern or book project states exactly how many beads are required, it is always best to buy more than specified if possible. This is particularly important with small seed beads. You may have to discard some beads as you work, perhaps because they are sharp-edged or misshapen, or you may break or lose some. Beads are made and dyed in batches, so if you have to buy more beads to finish a piece, you may well find that the new beads vary in color from those in the rest of the project. It may also take some time before your bead stockist has more supplies, or a color may occasionally be discontinued.

Decorative beads

As well as using seed beads, the projects in this book feature a variety of other decorative beads. These include wooden beads for the buckled satchel (project 6), a large round glass bead for the corsage on the dotty denim bag (project 10), drop-shaped lamp beads for the luxurious beaded wrap (project 15), teardrop beads for the jeweled scented sachets (project 19), and large luster-finished beads for the circular suede pillow (project 20).

Sequins

Sequins create an effect like fish scales on the surface of the knitted fabric, and working with them is very much like working with beads. They come in a variety of shapes, sizes, and finishes, and are usually made of plastic, so dry clean with care and avoid pressing because this tarnishes their appearance.

Circular sequins usually have a central hole; shaped sequins, such as the oval ones used in the sequined flapper bag (project 8), have a small hole at the top. Circular sequins can be either flat or cupped—that is, the edges are faceted and tilt up toward the central hole. Take care when using the cupped variety that they all face in the same direction (away from the surface of the knitting looks best).

As with beads, make sure that the hole in the sequin in large enough to accommodate a doubled end of yarn.

Tools

All you need to get started is a pair of needles and, as long as they are the right size for the project you are making, you can start knitting. However, there are many other items of equipment that you may find useful.

Needles

Needles are available in a variety of materials; the cheapest are aluminum and plastic. They can also be made from bamboo, steel, ebony, or even bone. Different materials will give you a different knitting experience, and personal preference will dictate which you choose to knit with. The important thing is that they are not bent and do not snag the yarn while knitting. The thickness or size of a needle should also be appropriate for the yarn you are using. A needle gauge is a handy and inexpensive tool to double-check the sizes of unmarked or old needles. There are three types of needle: straight, circular, and double pointed.

Straight needles

These come in pairs and vary from 10 to 18" (25 to 45 cm) in length. Make sure that the needle you are using is long enough for the width of the project. All of the projects in this book are knitted using pairs of straight needles.

Circular needles

These consist of two short needle ends joined by a flexible plastic or nylon cord. They come in different sizes and the length of cord varies. Although normally used for working in the round, circular needles can also be used for straight knitting, which is especially useful when you have too many stitches for a straight needle or your work is too heavy. They are used in this book for knitting the long hip ties for the lacy hip-tie v-neck (project 14).

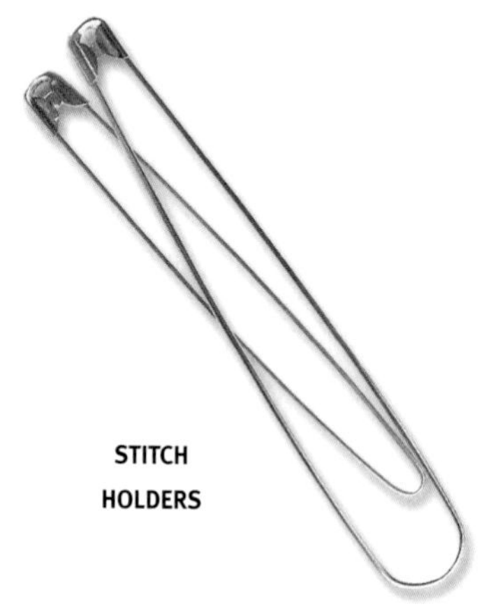

Double-pointed needles

These come in sets of four or five and are generally used for knitting socks and gloves. Having points at each end, they enable you to knit from either end of the needle. Two double-pointed needles are used in this book to knit i-cords for the floral striped bolster (project 17).

Stitch holders

Like large safety pins, these are used to hold stitches that have not been bound off so that they can be worked on later.

Tape measure

This is an essential piece of equipment for checking gauge and making sure that your work is the correct size.

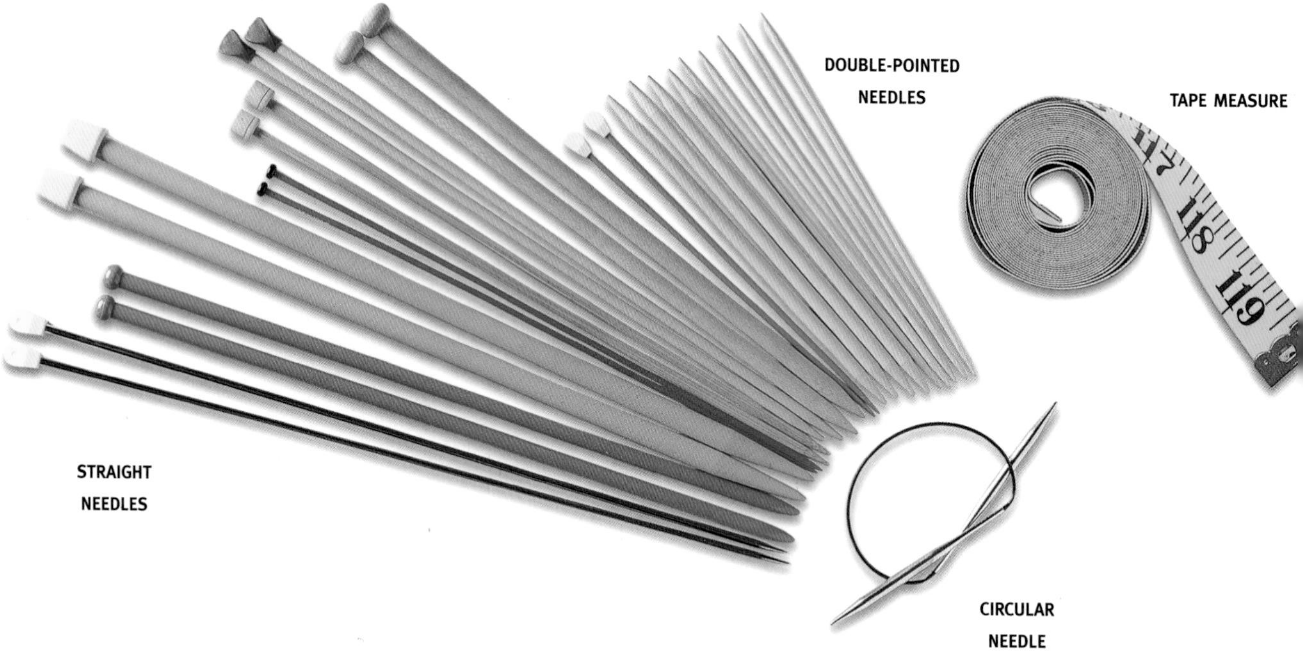

DOUBLE-POINTED NEEDLES

TAPE MEASURE

STRAIGHT NEEDLES

CIRCULAR NEEDLE

TIP: SAVE SCRAPS OF THREAD
Save scraps of sewing thread on half-empty reels and use them when threading beads and sequins onto yarn.

POINT PROTECTORS

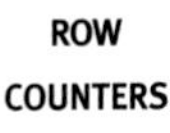
ROW COUNTERS

LIDDED CONTAINER

SCISSORS

Row counter
Place this on the end of a needle and turn the dial after each row to keep count of the number of rows worked.

Glass-headed pins
Glass-headed dressmaking pins are used to hold pieces of knitted fabric at the correct size before steaming.

Stitch markers
These colored plastic or metal rings can be placed onto a needle or into a stitch to mark a particular stitch or row. You could use scraps of contrasting colored yarn tied into a slipknot instead.

GLASS-HEADED PINS

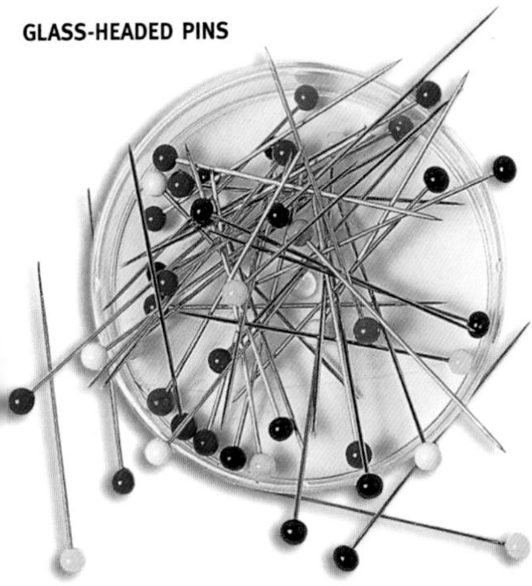

Scissors
These are essential for trimming the ends of yarn, particularly at the back of work, although it is better to break woolen yarns because the feathered ends from breaking are easier to hide when weaving in.

Sewing needles
Blunt-ended yarn needles come with different size eyes to accommodate various thicknesses of yarn. They are essential for weaving in loose ends of yarn and sewing seams. Sharp sewing needles are useful for threading beads and sequins onto yarn, or sewing them onto projects after knitting.

Crochet hook
This is handy for picking up stitches and adding tassel fringing to the edges of a piece of knitting.

Point protectors
Place these on the ends of needles when not in use to stop stitches from dropping off or to protect the tips of bamboo needles, which can chip or split.

Lidded containers
These are handy for storing your beads and sequins.

Small plate or tray
Use this when threading beads or sequins onto yarn for catching any spillages.

TIP: KEEPING A RECORD
Keep a small notebook handy to record yarns used, dye lots, personal gauge, felting notes, size of beads and sequins, and so on.

CROCHET HOOK

STITCH MARKERS

SEWING NEEDLES

Getting started

When learning or practicing basic techniques, choose a medium-weight yarn such as DK. This will help you feel that you are making some progress without having to work on too large a needle size.

Holding the yarn

There are numerous ways of holding the yarn; the best is the one that feels most comfortable. Those shown here leave your fingertips free to control the needles and tension the yarn so that it pulls quite tight as it passes through your hands.

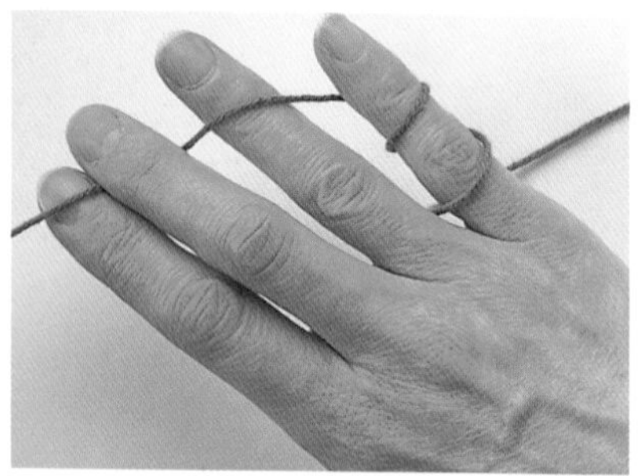

Right hand

Wrap the yarn around the little finger, then snake it over the ring finger, under the middle finger, and over the index finger.

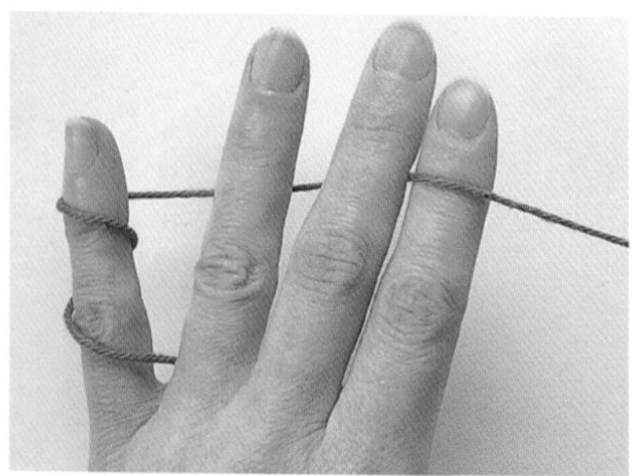

Left hand

Holding the yarn in this hand is faster because the yarn does not have as far to travel to work each stitch. Wrap the yarn around the little finger, then snake it around the other fingers in a way that feels comfortable.

Holding the needles

Needles can be held from above, known as the "knife hold," or from beneath, known as the "pen hold." The left needle is always held from above, while the right needle can be held either way.

American method

With this method, both needles are held from above in the knife hold. The right hand controls the yarn and moves the right needle into and out of the stitches on the left needle, while the left hand moves the stitches on the left needle.

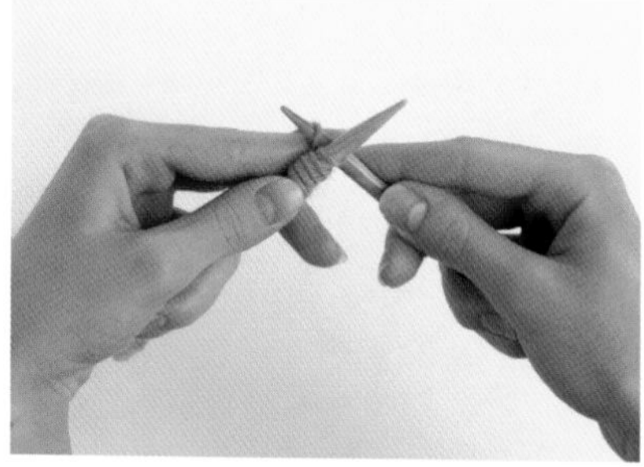

Continental method

This is the fastest method of knitting. Both the needles are held from above in the knife hold. The left hand controls the yarn and moves the stitches on the left needle, while the right hand moves the right needle into and out of the stitches on the left needle.

Scottish method

With this method, both needles are held from above in the knife hold. The left hand controls the needles, moving the stitches toward the tip of the left needle to be worked and guiding the right needle into and out of the stitches. The right needle is supported under the right arm, while the right hand controls the feed of the yarn.

French method

This style of knitting is considered to be elegant but time-consuming. The left needle is held from above in the knife hold, while the right needle is held from beneath in the pen hold between the thumb and index finger. The right index finger is used to guide the yarn around the needles.

Casting on

All knitting starts with a foundation row called a cast-on and this begins with a stitch called a slipknot. There are various ways of casting on, some of which are best suited to certain stitches, but generally it is a matter of personal preference.

Making a slipknot

Make a slipknot and place it on the left needle to form the first cast-on stitch.

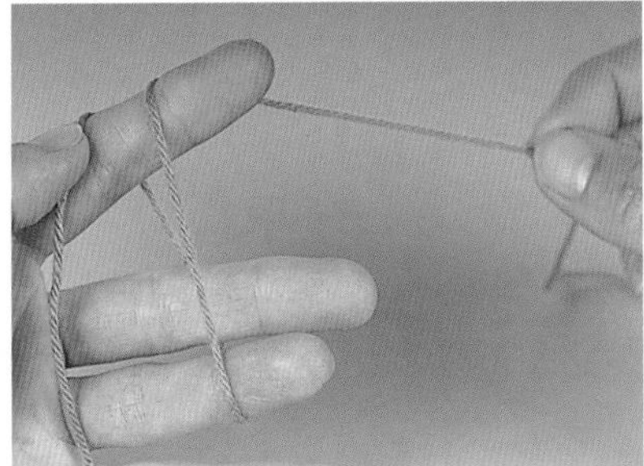

1 Make a loop by wrapping the yarn in a clockwise direction around the first three fingers of your left hand.

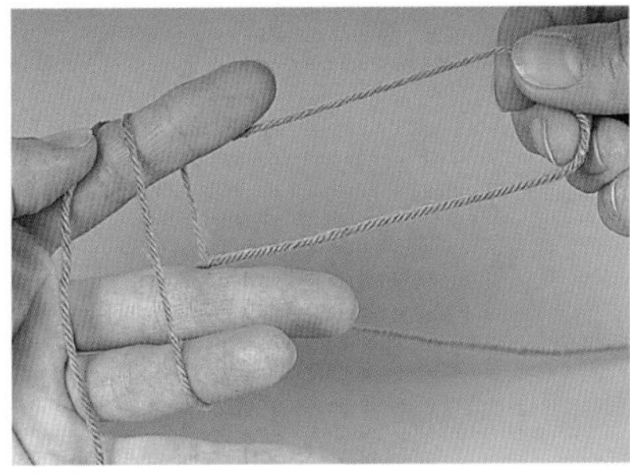

2 Pass the yarn held in your right hand under this loop to form another loop.

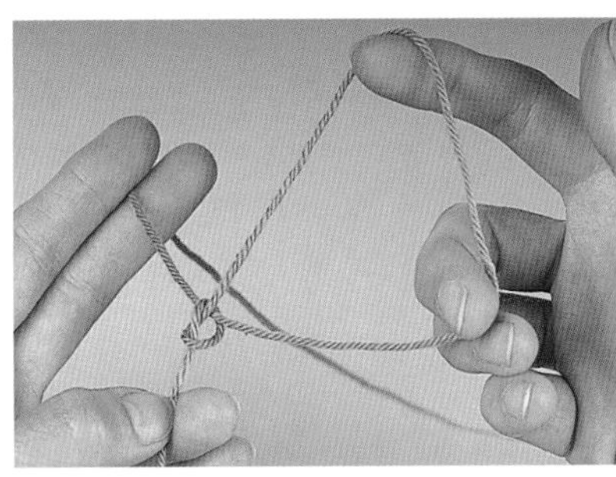

3 Remove your left hand from the first loop and pull the ends to tighten.

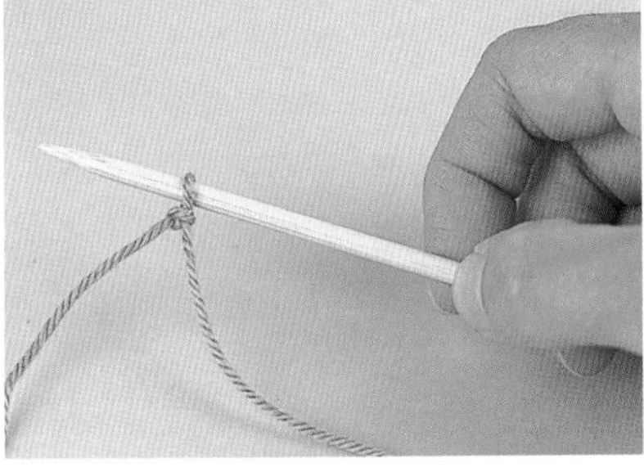

4 Place the loop from your right hand onto the needle and tighten. Do not pull too tight.

Cable cast-on

This popular cast-on method uses two needles and creates a firm but elastic edge that is suitable for most purposes.

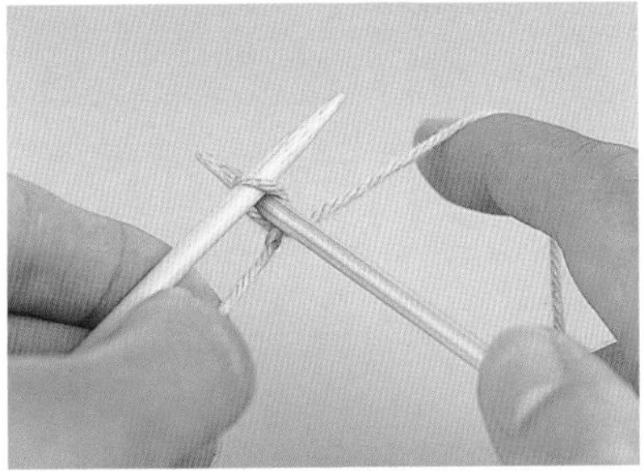

1 Make a slipknot and place it on the left needle. Insert the tip of the right needle into the slipknot from front to back underneath the left needle.

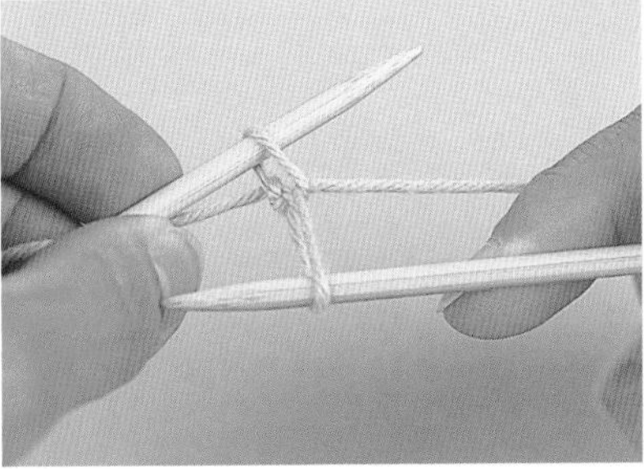

2 Wrap the yarn counterclockwise around the tip of the right needle. Pull the right needle back through the slipknot, drawing the yarn through the slipknot to make a new stitch.

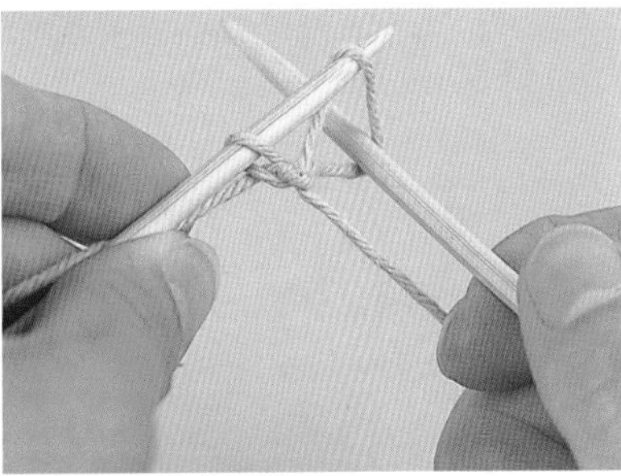

3 Transfer this stitch from the right needle to the left. Gently pull the long end of the yarn (the working yarn) to tighten the stitch around the needle.

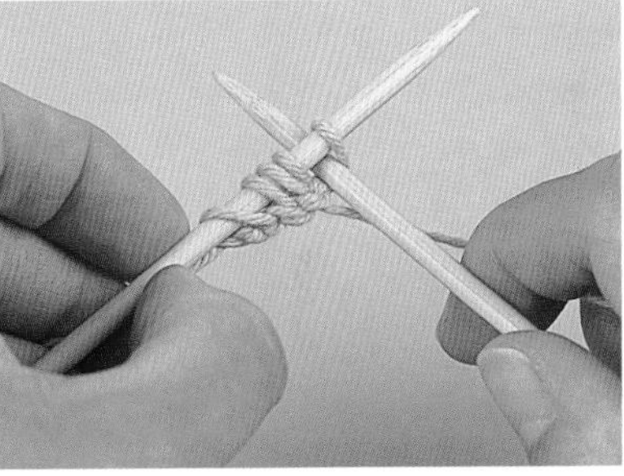

4 Use the same process to make as many stitches as required, but from now on insert the tip of the right needle between the top two stitches on the left needle. Transfer each new stitch to the left needle as before.

TIP: CORRECTING A TIGHT OR LOOSE CAST-ON

If your cast-on is too tight, insert the right needle between the first two stitches on the left needle before you tighten the yarn of the previous stitch to help prevent the cast-on from becoming too tight. Or, try casting on with a larger needle. If your cast-on is too loose, try casting on with a smaller needle. When knitting the first row after casting on, it sometimes helps to knit into the back of the stitches. This tightens up the cast-on edge.

Knit and purl

All knitted fabrics, no matter how complicated or simple, are based on two stitches: knit and purl. Always hold the yarn at the back of the work for a knit stitch and at the front of the work for a purl stitch unless instructed otherwise in the pattern (yb indicates that you should take the yarn to the back of the work, yf indicates that you should bring the yarn to the front of the work).

Knit stitch

Cast on the required number of stitches and hold the yarn at the back of the work. As you work across a row, the stitches will move from the left to the right needle. At the end of the row, swap the needles so that the needle with the stitches is in your left hand and the empty needle is in your right hand, ready to work the next row.

1 Insert the tip of the right needle into the stitch on the left needle from front to back underneath the left needle.

2 Wrap the yarn counterclockwise around the tip of the right needle.

3 Use the right needle to pull the wrapped yarn through the stitch on the left needle to create a new stitch on the right needle. Slip the original stitch off the left needle.

Purl stitch

Cast on the required number of stitches and hold the yarn at the front of the work. As with knit stitch, swap the needles when you reach the end of the row.

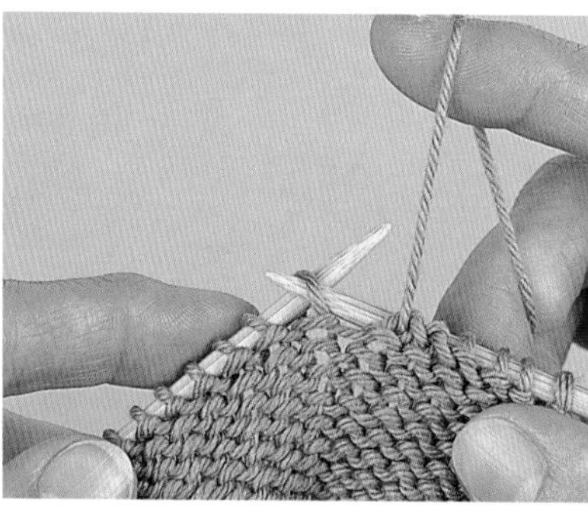

1 Insert the tip of the right needle into the stitch on the left needle from back to front underneath the left needle.

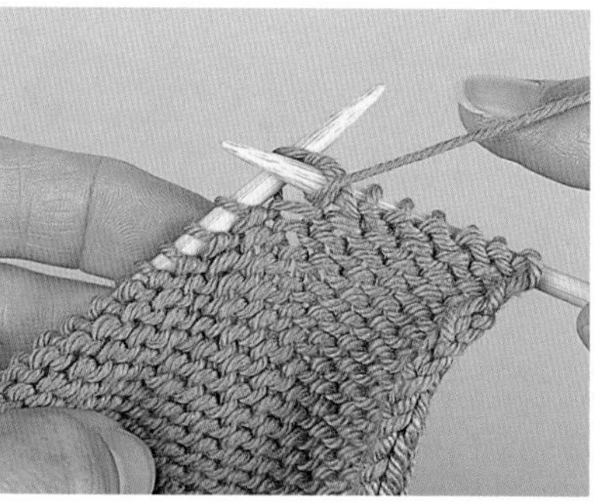

2 Wrap the yarn counterclockwise around the tip of the right needle.

3 Use the right needle to pull the wrapped yarn through the stitch on the left needle to create a new stitch on the right needle. Slip the original stitch off the left needle.

TIP: COUNTING ROWS

When you swap the needles at the end of each row, mark off the row you have just finished in the pattern or use a row counter to keep count of where you are.

Stitch patterns

By combining knit and purl stitches in different ways, you can create a variety of textured fabrics. The most frequently used are garter stitch, stockinette stitch, reverse stockinette stitch, seed stitch, and rib.

Garter stitch

Garter stitch is the simplest stitch pattern because it is created by either knitting or purling all the stitches on every row. The fabric it produces is springy and dense in texture and when pressed remains flat. This makes it ideal for use on edges.

Stockinette stitch

Stockinette stitch is the most well-known stitch pattern and is created by alternating knit and purl rows. This produces a more noticeable difference between the front or knit side, which is smooth, and the back or purl side, which has a more ridged appearance.

Reverse stockinette stitch

This is the same as stockinette stitch but uses the ridged purl side as the right side of the fabric.

Seed stitch

This is created by alternating knit and purl stitches on each row, with stitches that are knitted on right side rows also being knitted on wrong side rows, and the same with purl stitches. The fabric created is firm in texture like garter stitch and remains flat after pressing or steaming.

TIP: RIGHT SIDE/WRONG SIDE

Strictly speaking, the right and wrong side of the fabric depends on the stitch pattern you are using. With stockinette stitch, for example, the right side is the smooth face of the fabric and the ridged surface is the wrong side. However, in the case of garter stitch, both sides are the same. All of the patterns in this book tell you which side is the right side for each project.

TIP: TAKING A BREAK

Try not to put down a piece of work in the middle of a row because stitches can become stretched and create an uneven gauge. If you have left a piece of work for more than a week, unravel the last row. Sometimes stitches left on the needle for too long can create a ridge in the fabric.

Rib

This stitch makes a very elastic fabric that is mainly used for neckbands and edges. It is worked by alternating knit and purl stitches along each row to produce vertical lines of stitches on both sides of the work. The two most common ribs are single rib and double rib.

1 Single rib is worked as k1, p1 all across each row.

2 Double rib is worked as k2, p2 all across each row.

Binding off

Once you have finished your knitting, you need to secure the stitches by binding them off. Binding off is also used to finish a group of stitches to shape the work. The bound-off edge should stretch about as much as the rest of the knitting.

Binding off knitwise

Throughout the projects, you will be instructed to bind off knitwise, purlwise, or in pattern.

1 Knit the first two stitches from the left needle onto the right needle in the usual way. *With the yarn at the back of the work, insert the tip of the left needle into the front of the first of these knitted stitches, from left to right.

2 Lift this stitch over the second stitch and slip it off the right needle so that you have only one stitch on the right needle.

3 Knit the next stitch on the left needle so that there are two stitches on the right needle once again. Repeat from * until you reach the last stitch.

4 Break off the yarn, leaving a tail of about 6" (15 cm). Slip the final stitch off the right needle, thread the tail of yarn through it, and pull tight to secure. The bind-off looks like a chain along the top of the knitting, which is why this method is sometimes called chain bind-off.

TIP: COUNTING THE BIND-OFF
When binding off a certain number of stitches, such as for shaping a neck, count the stitches as you lift them off the needle, not as you work them. The stitch remaining on the right needle does not count as a bound-off stitch.

Binding off purlwise

When binding off purl stitches, simply purl the first two stitches as usual and follow the instructions for binding off knitwise, purling stitches instead of knitting them and keeping the yarn at the front of the work. To lift each stitch off the right needle, insert the left needle into the back of the stitch, from left to right.

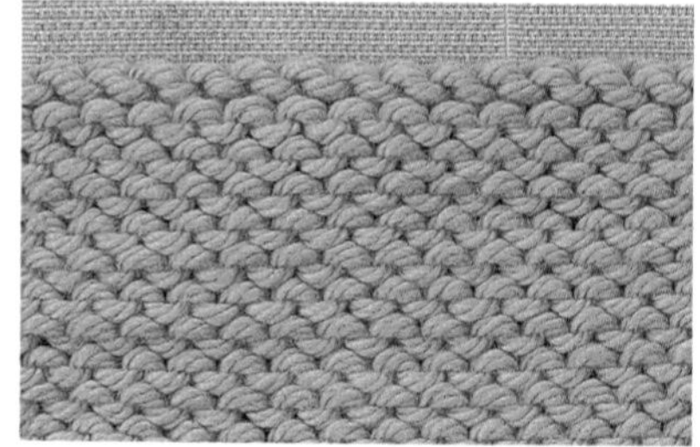

Binding off in pattern

Sometimes a pattern will instruct you to bind off in pattern. This means that you should bind off all knit stitches knitwise and all purl stitches purlwise. For example, if the pattern is double rib, as shown below, bind off two stitches knitwise, then two stitches purlwise, and so on.

Gauge

Most knitting patterns specify an ideal gauge, which is the number of stitches and rows counted over a certain measurement, usually 4" (10 cm) square, worked in a specified stitch pattern and needle size. If you do not work to the correct gauge, the knitting will end up the wrong size. This is not important for some projects, but is crucial when knitting items such as garments.

Making a test swatch

It is always advisable to knit a small swatch to measure your gauge and compare it to that stated in the pattern. The instructions will indicate the recommended needle size and what type of stitch pattern the gauge has been measured over.

Using the recommended needle size, cast on the number of stitches specified in the gauge guide plus four more. If the stitches are to be measured over a pattern, cast on the correct multiple of stitches to knit the pattern. Work in the required pattern until the swatch measures approximately 5" (12.5 cm) square. Cut the yarn, thread it through the stitches, and slip them off the needle. Do not pull the yarn tight or bind off because this may distort the stitches. Measure the gauge as follows.

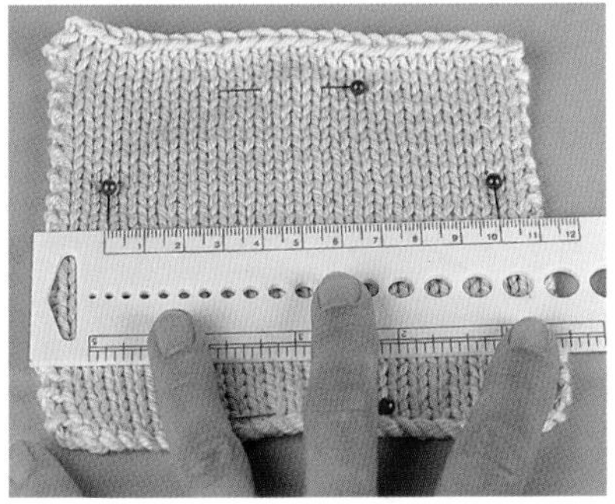

1 Lay the swatch on a flat surface. Placing a ruler in the center of the swatch, measure 4" (10 cm) horizontally and vertically across the knitting. Mark each of these distances with two pins.

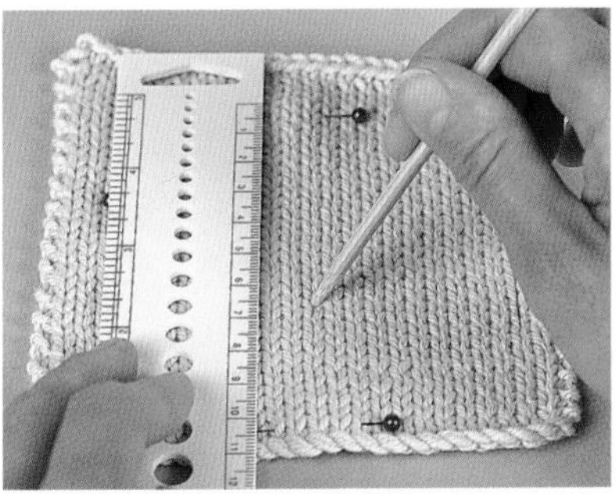

2 Use the tip of a knitting needle to count the number of stitches and rows between the pins, including half stitches.

Adjusting your gauge

If you have fewer stitches than stated in the gauge guide, your knitting is too loose and the garment will be too big. Knit another swatch using smaller needles. If you have more stitches than stated in the gauge guide, your knitting is too tight and the garment will be too small. Knit another swatch using larger needles. This should give you the correct gauge if you are off by only one or two stitches. However, if the difference is greater, you may need to adjust the size of garment that you make.

TIP: A LITTLE DIFFERENCE CAN GO A LONG WAY

You may feel that knitting a test swatch is a waste of time but remember that it could well save you from reknitting or abandoning a project or being disappointed with the end result. Knitting is an individual craft—we do not all knit to the same gauge. Although a difference of two or three stitches may seem minor, remember that this is two or three stitches in just 4" (10 cm). Think how many 4" (10 cm) there are across the width of your garment. For example, if the gauge should be 20 stitches and yours is 22 stitches to 4" (10 cm), a garment measuring 24" (60 cm) has six lots of 4" (10 cm), so your garment will be off by 12 stitches. This means your garment will only measure approximately 22" (55 cm) and could be too small or an uncomfortable fit.

Too tight **Correct gauge** **Too loose**

Patterns and charts

The instructions for knitting a project may be provided in either written or chart form. Always read the whole pattern before you start knitting to ensure that you have everything you need and understand all the instructions.

Essential information

All patterns provide a list containing the size of the finished item, the materials and needles required, the gauge of the piece, and the abbreviations used in the instructions. Although many abbreviations are standardized, such as k for knit and p for purl, some of them vary, so always read the abbreviations in each pattern before you start knitting.

Abbreviations

Abbreviations are used to save space and make written patterns easier to follow. The abbreviations used in this book are:

bead	place specified number of beads at front of knitting and then slip specified number of stitches purlwise
fringe 1	make 1 beaded fringe
k	knit
k1f&b	knit into front and back of stitch
m1	make 1 stitch by picking up horizontal bar before next stitch and knitting or purling into back of it as instructed
ML	make loop
p	purl
p1f&b	purl into front and back of stitch
psso	pass slip stitch over
RS	right side
seq 1	place 1 sequin and slip 1 stitch purlwise
skpo	slip 1 stitch, knit 1 stitch, pass slip stitch over
s2kpo	slip 2 stitches, knit 1 stitch, pass slip stitches over
sl	slip specified number of stitches knitwise or purlwise as instructed
ssk	slip 1 stitch, slip 1 stitch, knit both stitches on right needle by inserting tip of left needle through front of both loops
st(s)	stitch(es)
tbl	through back of loop
tog	together
WS	wrong side
yb	take yarn between needles to back of work as if to knit
yf	bring yarn between needles to front of work as if to purl
yo	yarn over

The floral summer throw (project 18) is created by repeating various sections of the pattern in different colors.

Repeats

When following the pattern instructions, you will find that some of them appear within curved parentheses and some are marked with an asterisk. Instructions that appear within parentheses are to be repeated. For example, instead of writing "p2, k2, p2, k2," the pattern will simply say "(p2, k2) twice." Asterisks (*) indicate the point to which you should return when you reach the phrase "repeat from *." They may also mark whole sets of instructions that are to be repeated. For example, "repeat from * to **" means repeat the instructions between the single and double asterisks.

Charts are ideal when knitting items with multiple colors, such as the optic-striped pillow (project 16), because you can see at a glance where color changes need to occur.

Garments, such as the beaded float skirt (project 11), are provided in several sizes.

Sizing

Most garment patterns are written for more than one size; in this book the smallest size is shown first, with subsequent sizes in brackets—for example, small [medium, large]. This format is repeated throughout a pattern for all the sets of figures that differ from one size to the next—for example, the number of stitches to cast on. Follow the instructions for the size you are making. Where only one figure is given, this applies to all sizes. Some of the patterns in this book have separate instructions for each size in order to make them easier for beginners to follow.

> **TIP: HIGHLIGHT YOUR SIZE**
> When knitting a garment that has instructions for different sizes in brackets, you may find it easier to follow if you highlight the relevant instructions for the particular size you are making.

Charts

Charts are a graphic representation of your knitting, with each square representing one stitch and each horizontal line representing one row. All charts have a key nearby to explain each of the symbols and/or colors used. Charts have several advantages over row-by-row written instructions: you can see where you are at a glance; you learn to plan ahead, especially in color knitting; and they help to increase your understanding of knitting. Always remember that charts are read from the bottom up. Right side (RS) rows are read from right to left; wrong side (WS) rows are read from left to right. The chart indicates how the work appears on the right side.

KEY

- k on RS, p on WS
- bead 1
- sl 1 purlwise on RS, sl 1 knitwise on WS
- A—lilac
- B—purple
- C—cream
- D—blue

> **TIP: ENLARGING CHARTS**
> If you are new to working from charts, you may find it helpful to enlarge them on a photocopier to make them easier to follow. It is also a good idea to mark off each row as you go.

Shaping

There are lots of different ways of increasing or decreasing the number of stitches in order to shape a piece of knitting. The method you use will depend on the number of stitches that need to be increased or decreased, and where in the pattern the shaping is required.

Increasing

The projects in this book use several methods to increase 1 stitch at a time (k1f&b, p1f&b, m1), plus the cable increase technique for increasing multiple stitches.

K1f&b

Work to the point in the row where you need to increase. Knit into the front of the stitch on the left needle in the usual way, but do not slip it off the left needle when you have finished. Keeping the original stitch on the left needle and the yarn at the back of the work, knit into the back of the stitch—you have now increased one stitch. Slip the stitch from the left needle.

P1f&b

Work this in the same way as k1f&b, but purl into the front and back of the stitch instead of knitting into it, with the yarn at the front of the work.

M1 knitwise

This increase uses the horizontal bar that lies between pairs of stitches to make a new stitch. It can be worked anywhere on a row and creates an invisible increase. The pattern will specify whether to make the stitch knitwise or purlwise.

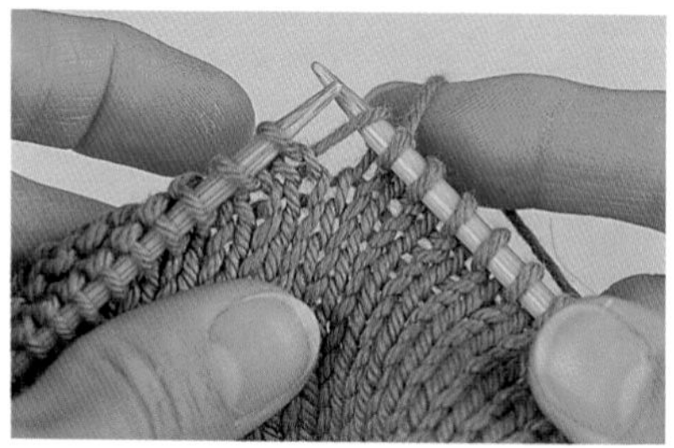

1 Work to the point where you need to increase. Insert the tip of the right needle underneath the horizontal bar lying between the last stitch on the right needle and the first stitch on the left needle.

2 Lift this bar and slip it onto the left needle. Knit into the back of this loop to create a new stitch, slipping the lifted loop off the left needle when you have finished.

M1 purlwise

Repeat steps 1 and 2 of make 1 knitwise, but purl into the back of the lifted loop instead of knitting into it.

Cable increase

It is sometimes necessary to increase multiple stitches. Insert the right needle between the top two stitches on the left needle, then cast on the number of stitches specified in the pattern using the cable cast-on technique.

TIP: WORK ONE STITCH IN

Work increases and decreases one stitch in from the edges of the fabric to create a neater edge and make sewing seams and picking up stitches easier and neater.

Decreasing

The projects use several methods of decreasing stitches. Note that the techniques for working two stitches together (k2tog, k2tog tbl, p2tog, p2tog tbl) can also be used to work more than two stitches together in order to decrease a greater number of stitches.

K2tog

Knit 2 together creates a slope to the right on the face of the fabric. Work to where you need to decrease, then insert the right needle knitwise into the front of the first two stitches on the left needle. Knit the stitches together as if they were a single stitch. You have now decreased one stitch.

K2tog tbl

Knit 2 together through the back of the loop creates a slope to the left on the face of the fabric. Work to where you need to decrease, then insert the right needle knitwise into the back of the first two stitches on the left needle. Knit the stitches together as if they were a single stitch. You have now decreased one stitch.

P2tog

Purl 2 together creates a slope to the right on the face of the fabric. Work as for k2tog, but purl the stitches together instead of knitting them.

P2tog tbl

Purl 2 together through the back of the loop creates a slope to the left on the face of the fabric. Work as for k2tog tbl, but purl the stitches together through the back of the loop instead of knitting them.

Ssk

This decrease creates a slope to the left on the face of the fabric. Slip two stitches knitwise, one at a time, from the left to the right needle. Insert the left needle through the front loop of both stitches, then knit them together from this position.

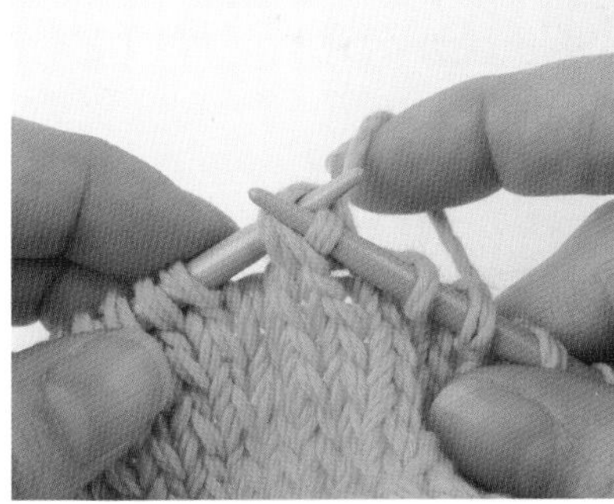

Slip stitch decreasing (skpo, s2kpo)

Skpo (slip 1, knit 1, pass slip stitch over) is a method of decreasing that is often used when making lace holes. It creates a slope to the left on the face of the fabric. Slip one stitch knitwise from the left to the right needle without working it. Knit the next stitch on the left needle in the usual way, then use the left needle to lift the slip stitch over the knit stitch and drop it off the right needle. The variation shown above, s2kpo (slip 2, knit 1, pass both slip stitches over), is used in the lacy hip-tie v-neck (project 14).

Bind-off decrease

This decrease is usually done at the beginning of a row. Simply work to where you need to decrease, then bind off the number of stitches specified in the pattern in the usual way. If you are instructed to do it in the middle of a row, you will need to rejoin the yarn to the stitches before the bind-off in order to continue working them.

Other stitch techniques

Having learned the basics of knitting, purling, and shaping, you will find that there are many variations on these instructions used in knitting patterns to create specific effects.

Joining new yarn

Whenever a ball of yarn is about to run out, join a new one at the beginning of a row. When possible, avoid joining a new ball of yarn in the middle of a row.

1 To help keep good tension when starting a new yarn, tie it around the original yarn. Without breaking or cutting the yarn used for the previous row, tie the new yarn around the end of the old yarn, leaving a 6" (15 cm) tail.

2 Slide the knot up to the next stitch and work the row using the new yarn. Hold the tail of yarn out of the way for the first few stitches, then break or cut the old yarn, leaving a 6" (15 cm) tail. When you have finished the piece, untie the knot and weave in the ends of yarn.

Holding stitches

Some projects require stitches to be left on a stitch holder and worked at a later stage in the pattern.

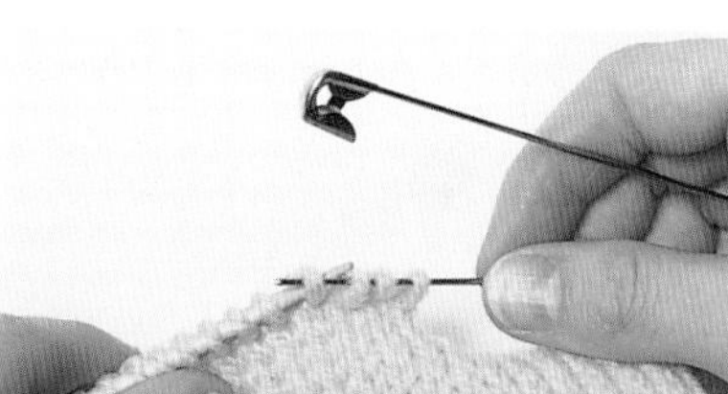

1 To transfer stitches to a stitch holder, simply insert the pin of the holder from right to left through each stitch on the left needle, or from left to right through each stitch on the right needle, taking care not to twist them.

2 Close the holder. The stitches will not unravel. When you need to work on these stitches again, slip them from the holder onto a knitting needle, taking care not to twist them.

Slipping stitches

Many techniques involve slipping stitches from one needle to another without working them.

Knitwise

To slip a stitch knitwise, insert the tip of the right needle into the stitch on the left needle as if to knit it. Slip the stitch from the left to the right needle without working into it.

Purlwise

To slip a stitch purlwise, insert the tip of the right needle into the stitch on the left needle as if to purl it. Slip the stitch from the left to the right needle without working into it.

Yarn overs

This involves taking the yarn over the right needle to create a lace hole.

1 This example shows a yarn over between two knit stitches. Instead of knitting the second stitch with the yarn at the back of the work in the usual way, bring the yarn forward between the needles to the front of the work, then wrap it over the right needle to knit the stitch.

2 This yarn over is between two purl stitches. Instead of purling the second stitch with the yarn at the front of the work in the usual way, take the yarn between the needles to the back of the work, then wrap it over the right needle to purl the stitch.

3 This example shows a yarn over between a knit and a purl stitch. Bring the yarn between the needles to the front of the work, then take the yarn over the right needle to the back, then between the needles to the front again, and purl the next stitch as usual.

4 This yarn over is between a purl and a knit stitch. After purling the first stitch, leave the yarn in front of the work, then knit the next stitch, taking the yarn over and toward the back of the right needle as the next stitch is knit.

Chain stitch

This decorative stitch is used to create the motifs on the luxurious beaded wrap (project 15) using four ends of yarn.

1 Bring the needle through to the front of the knitted fabric, then take it to the back at the same point where you brought it to the front, creating a loop.

2 Bring the needle through to the front where you want the chain stitch to end. Take it through the center of the loop and then to the back of the knitted fabric at the same point.

3 Tighten the stitch to neaten it. Sew as many chain stitches as required to create the shape of the motif.

Picking up stitches

Many knitted pieces have a border of some kind to neaten the edge and prevent the fabric from curling. These can be knitted separately and sewn onto the piece, or they can be worked by picking up stitches along the edge and working them. Stitches must be picked up evenly, particularly around areas such as necklines that will be a focal point. You can pick up stitches using a knitting needle or a crochet hook. For a neater appearance, use a knitting needle or crochet hook one or two sizes smaller than the project size to pick up the stitches. If the border is worked in another color than the body of the piece, it can look better if you pick up the stitches in the main color and then change yarn colors for the first row.

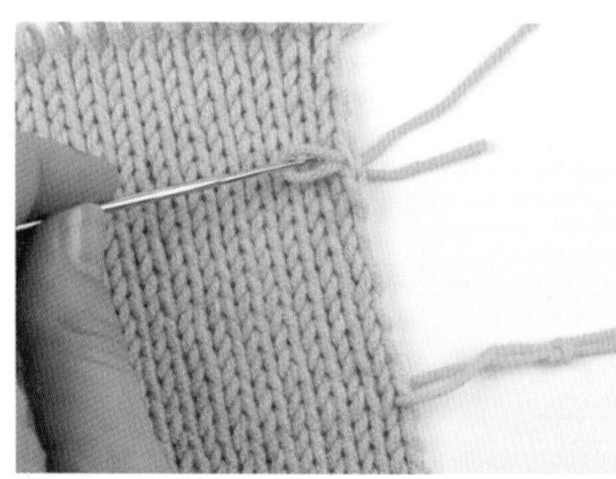

Marking the edge

Measure the edge of the knitted piece and place markers or short knotted pieces of yarn at regular intervals, such as every 2" (5 cm). To calculate how many stitches to pick up between the markers, divide the number of stitches required by the number of sections. For example, if you need to pick up 20 stitches along a 10" (25 cm) edge that has been divided into five 2" (5 cm) sections, you will need to pick up four stitches in each section.

Along a horizontal edge

When picking up stitches along a horizontal edge, insert the tip of the right needle into the center of the first full stitch below the bind-off row. Do not pick up stitches in the bind-off row, otherwise the pick-up row may appear to be a half-stitch off when compared to stitches in the rows below. When picking up stitches along the cast-on edge, work the pick-up one full row above the cast-on edge, or as specified in the instructions.

1 With the right side of the work facing you, insert the right needle (or crochet hook) from front to back through the center of the stitch.

2 Wrap the yarn around the needle as if to knit and pull the loop through to the front of the work to create a new stitch on the right needle. If using a crochet hook, slip the new loop onto the right needle. Do this for as many stitches as required.

Along a vertical edge

When picking up stitches along a vertical edge, work one full stitch in from the edge of the knitted piece.

1 With the right side of the work facing you, insert the right needle from front to back into the first full stitch of the first row—that is, one whole stitch in from the edge.

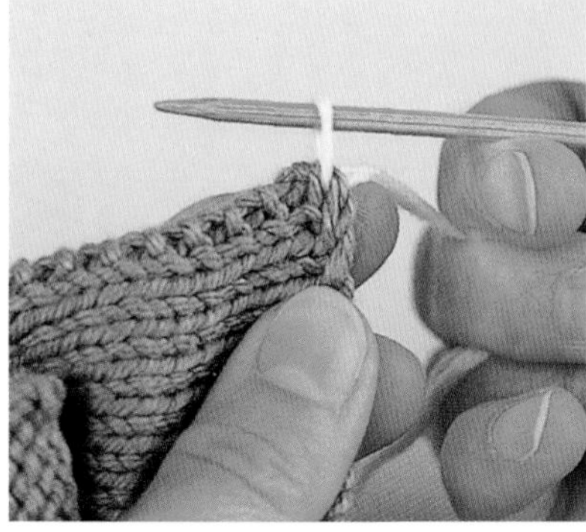

2 Wrap the yarn around the needle as if to knit and pull the loop through to the front of the work to create a new stitch on the right needle. Repeat for as many stitches as required.

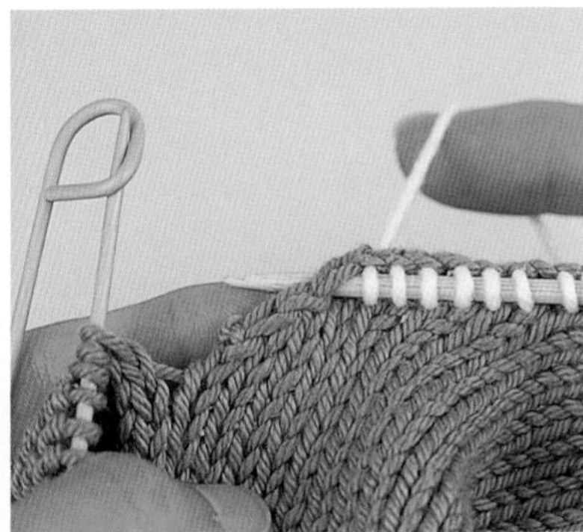

Along a shaped edge
When picking up stitches on any piece of shaped knitting, pick up one stitch in from the edge to eliminate jagged or untidy shaping. Follow the line of the curve, and avoid picking up stitches in any large gaps between bound-off stitches or decreases.

TIP: NEATENING LOOPY STITCHES
Stitches that were placed on stitch holders or not bound off (center front neckline, for example) are likely to have stretched loopy stitches at each end. To neaten these areas and prevent a hole, use one of the following methods. Work into the back loop of the offending stitch, thereby twisting it and tightening the stitch to match the others. Or, if the stitch is very loose, slip the stitch knitwise onto the right needle, insert the left needle from back to front under the running strand, pull up a loop, and slip it knitwise onto the right needle, then work both the stitch and loop together using the ssk decrease method.

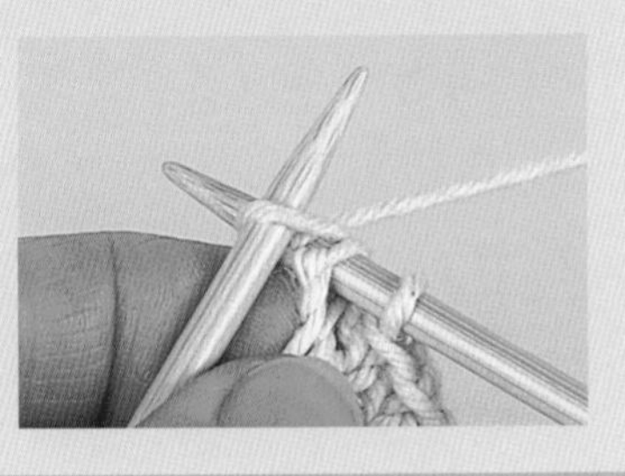

Making loops (ML)

Loops are a great way of adding texture and pattern to a design.

1 Knit one stitch, but do not slip it off the left needle. Bring the yarn between the needles to the front of the work.

2 Wrap the yarn clockwise around your thumb to form a loop of the length required, then take the yarn between the needles to the back of the work.

3 Knit into the same stitch again, this time slipping it off the left needle.

4 Bring the yarn between the needles to the front of the work and wrap it over the right needle to make one stitch.

5 Pass the two stitches just worked over this stitch.

6 Pull the loop around your thumb to tighten it, then slip it off your thumb. Continue along the row, forming as many loops as instructed in the pattern.

Knitting with beads and sequins

The key element in all of the projects in this book is the fact that they are embellished with beads, sequins, or both. Knitting with beads and sequins is very simple and even novice knitters can easily master the techniques.

Threading beads and sequins onto yarn

Beads and sequins must be threaded onto the yarn before casting on. You will need a sewing needle and a scrap of sewing thread.

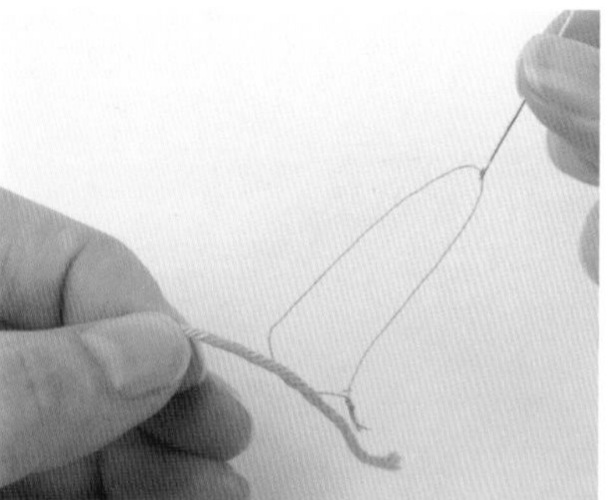

1 Thread a sewing needle that will easily pass through the beads or sequins with sewing thread. Knot the ends of the thread, then slip the end of the yarn through the loop of thread.

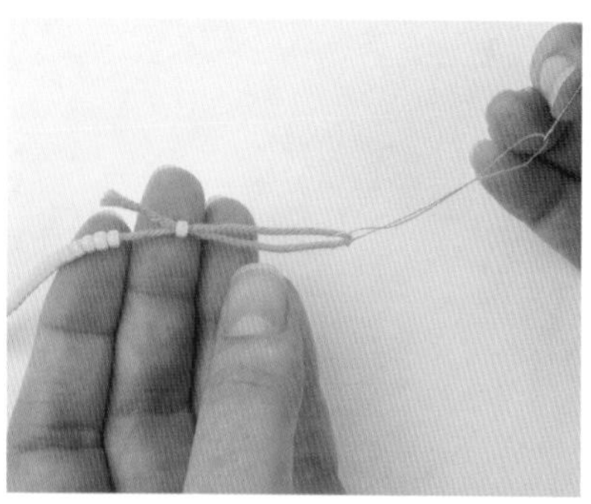

2 Slide each bead or sequin onto the needle, then down the thread and onto the yarn. Make sure that you thread them onto the yarn in the correct sequence if necessary.

Knitting with beads

Use this technique to add a sprinkling of beads to the surface of your knitting.

Placing 1 bead per stitch

Most of the projects in this book place beads in the knitting so that there is one bead in front of one stitch.

1 Work to the required position in the pattern and bring the yarn between the needles to the front of the work.

2 Push a bead up the yarn until it is in front of the right needle.

3 Slip the next stitch purlwise from the left to the right needle and bring the bead up to sit in front of the slip stitch.

4 Take the yarn between the needles to the back of the work, then continue the pattern.

TIP: THREADING SEQUENCE

When knitting with beads or sequins of more than one color or size, remember that the last bead or sequin that you thread on will be the first that you knit with, so thread them onto the yarn in the reverse order to the order in which you will be knitting them.

Beaded floats

Some patterns specify that you should place a greater number of beads at a particular point in the pattern, but still one bead per stitch. This is indicated clearly in the list of abbreviations for the particular project.

1 Push the specified number of beads up the yarn until they are in front of the right needle, then slip the same number of stitches purlwise.

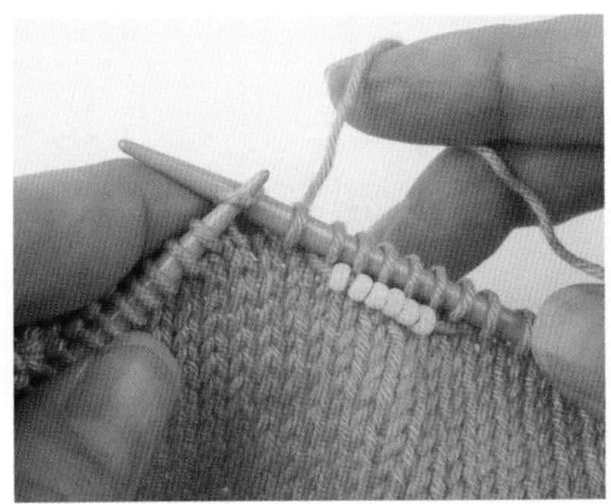

2 Take the yarn between the needles to the back of the work, then continue the pattern.

Placing 2 beads per stitch

Two of the projects in this book place two beads in front of a single stitch instead of the usual one bead. These are the funky felted belt (project 1) and the sumptuously soft shrug (project 12). This is indicated in the list of abbreviations for these projects.

1 Work to the required position in the pattern and bring the yarn between the needles to the front of the work. Push two beads up the yarn until they are in front of the right needle.

TIP: BEADING IN BATCHES

Too many pre-strung beads can make knitting difficult and affect the gauge, so it is a good idea to thread the beads onto the yarn in batches of 100 at a time. Break off the yarn to thread on more beads as necessary. In addition, you may well find that a ball of yarn runs out before all the beads have been used. This is because everyone knits to a slightly different gauge, making it impossible to predict exactly where in the pattern each ball of yarn will finish. You may therefore have to rethread any unused beads onto a new ball of yarn during knitting.

TIP: PULL TIGHTER

When knitting the stitch immediately after placing a bead or beads, pull a little tighter on the yarn than usual. This will ensure that the bar of yarn on which the bead sits is as short as possible, and will help stop the bead from slipping through to the other side of the work.

2 Slip the next stitch purlwise (just one stitch) and bring the beads up to sit in front of the slip stitch.

3 Take the yarn between the needles to the back of the work, then continue the pattern.

Knitting with sequins

Sequins can be added to a knitted fabric in the same way as beads, but they can be a little trickier to work with. You need to position them carefully because sequined knitting is difficult to unravel. In this book, only one sequin is ever placed at a time.

1 Work to the required position in the pattern and bring the yarn between the needles to the front of the work. Push one sequin up the yarn until it is in front of the right needle.

2 Slip the next stitch purlwise and bring the sequin up to sit in front of the slip stitch.

TIP: USING CUPPED SEQUINS

If you are using cupped sequins, make sure that the cupped side is facing toward the ball of yarn when you are threading them. This will ensure that the sequins all face away from the knitted fabric, giving the most attractive result.

3 Take the yarn between the needles to the back of the work, then continue the pattern.

Beaded fringe

The slouchy summer bag (project 7) is knitted with a beaded fringe on the front. The following demonstration shows how to work the instruction for "fringe 1."

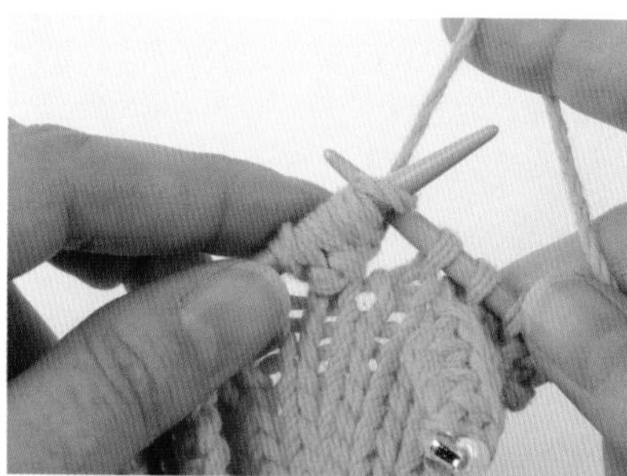

1 Work to the required position in the pattern. Cast on six stitches, then insert the right needle into the first stitch.

2 Push two beads up the yarn, then wrap the yarn around the right needle to knit this stitch, trapping the beads at the front of the work as you do so.

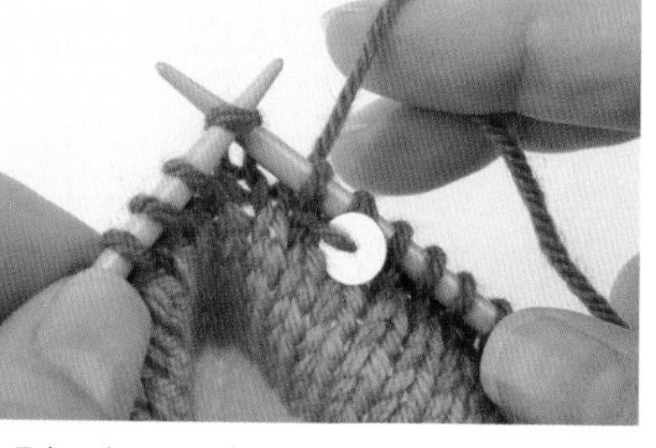

3 Pull the yarn tight and knit the next stitch so that you have two stitches on the right needle.

4 Lift the first stitch over the second to bind off one stitch.

5 Bind off the remaining extra stitches in the same way. Continue adding beaded fringes where indicated in the pattern.

Finishing

Now that you have completed your project, you have come to the task that a lot of knitters hate—weaving in ends, blocking and steaming, and sewing seams. Having knitted a project with such care, take your time. There are many finishing tips and techniques; the ones described here will help you with the projects in this book.

Weaving in ends

All pieces of knitting begin and end with a tail of yarn, and more are created when you join in a new ball, change colors, and sew seams. Always leave a 6" (15 cm) tail of yarn, so that it can be threaded into a yarn needle easily and woven into the wrong side of the knitted fabric. Undo any knots joining yarns, then thread the yarn end through a blunt-ended yarn needle.

Along a seam

Run the needle in and out of the stitches inside the seam at the edge of the knitting for about 3" (8 cm). Pull the yarn through and trim the end.

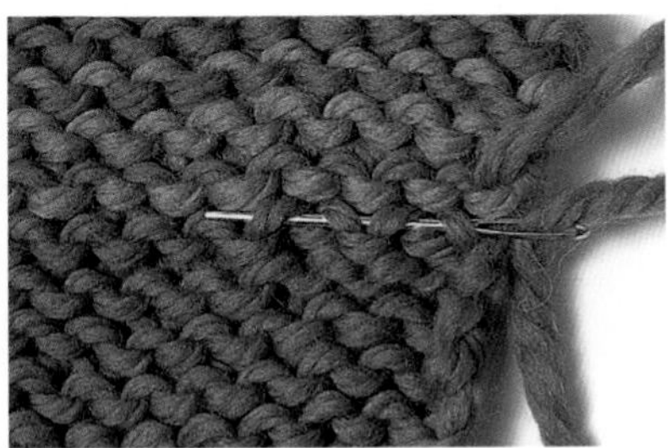

Along a row

1 Run the needle in and out of the back of stitches of the same color, working along the row for about 4–6 stitches.

2 Take the needle back, catching in the woven-in yarn for 2–3 stitches. Stretch the knitting widthwise and trim the end of the yarn.

Blocking and steaming

Blocking is the term used for pinning out each knitted piece to the correct size before steaming.

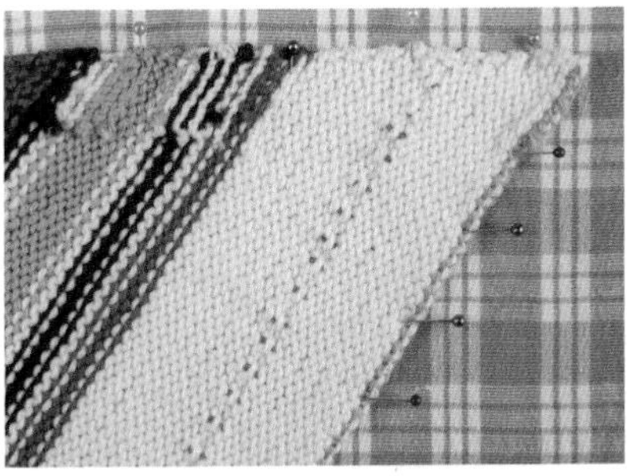

1 Check your pattern for the finished measurements. Using large glass-headed pins and with the wrong side of the knitting facing upward, pin the pieces out to the correct dimensions, taking care not to stretch the knitting out of shape.

2 Heat an iron to the steam setting, then place a slightly damp towel or thick cloth over the fabric. Holding the iron about 1" (2.5 cm) above the surface of the knitting, press the steam button and allow the steam to penetrate the fabric. Do not allow the iron to make contact with the knitted fabric to avoid tarnishing or melting any beads or sequins, or losing the elasticity in any ribbed or highly textured stitch patterns.

TIP: MAKING A BLOCKING BOARD

You can use an ironing board for blocking small pieces, or make a blocking board by covering a piece of hardboard with a layer of padding and an over-layer of cotton fabric. Stretch them tight across the board and secure them to the underside with staples, glue, or tape. Choose a checked fabric so that you can use the squares as a guide for pinning out pieces with the edges straight.

Sewing seams

There are several methods of sewing seams together. Overcasting, backstitch, and mattress stitch are used in this book. Use a blunt-ended yarn needle and matching colored yarn.

Overcasting

This is sometimes referred to as a flat seam because it produces a very narrow seam. Hold the edges of both pieces right sides together in one hand. With your other hand, insert the needle from the back of the work through the edge stitches of both pieces. Pull the yarn through to the front, then take it over the knitted edge and sew once again a few stitches along from where you started. Continue evenly along the edge and secure at both ends by weaving in the yarn ends.

> **TIP: NEVER SEW SEAMS WITH YARN ENDS**
>
> It is better to use a separate piece of yarn to sew seams rather than the tail left over from casting on. If you do make a mistake, it can be easily pulled out of the fabric rather than having to unpick it.

Backstitch

This creates a strong but non-elastic seam and is suitable where firmness is required and for light-weight yarns. It is worked with the wrong sides facing you, so it can be difficult to pattern match exactly. Pin the pieces right sides together, matching the pieces as closely as possible, and keep the stitches near the edge to avoid creating a bulky seam.

1 Secure the seam and yarn by taking the needle twice around the outer edges of the fabric, from back to front.

2 Take the yarn around the outside edge once more, but this time insert the needle through the work from back to front no more than ½" (1.3 cm) from where the yarn last came out.

3 Insert the needle from front to back at the point where the first stitch began, then bring the needle back through to the front, the same distance along the edge as before. Repeat this process along the whole seam, then secure the end with a couple of overlapping stitches.

4 The completed seam, when sewn in matching colored yarn, is strong and neat.

Mattress stitch

Also known as invisible stitch, this method can be used for any seam and creates a strong, neat, almost invisible join. It is worked with the fabrics laid flat and right sides facing you, so it is ideal when working in stripes or textured patterns because it is easy to pattern match.

1 It is important to get a neat bottom edge when joining seams. To do this, thread a needle with yarn and bring it through from the back as close to the bottom and side edges as possible. Make a figure eight with the yarn and needle by bringing it out from the right piece, under and through the left piece from back to front, and then under and through the right piece again from back to front.

2 Move across to the left piece and up through the same hole from which the yarn creating the figure eight comes.

3 From the front, insert the needle into either the middle or to the side of the next stitch up on the right-hand side. Point the needle up and bring it through to the front two stitches up, so that two bars of yarn lie across the needle.

4 From the front, insert the needle into either the middle or to the side of the next stitch up on the left-hand side. Point the needle up and bring it through to the front two stitches up, so that two bars of yarn lie across the needle.

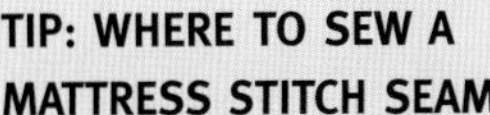

TIP: WHERE TO SEW A MATTRESS STITCH SEAM

Work a mattress stitch seam a half stitch in from the side edge when using heavier weight yarns in order to avoid bulky seams (as shown here); work a whole stitch in from the side edge when using light- and medium-weight yarns.

5 Continue zigzagging from one edge to the other until you have completed the seam. When finished, secure both ends of the seam with a couple of overlapping stitches. The seam should appear invisible from the right side.

TIP: AFTERCARE

Always refer to the instructions on the yarn ball band for guidelines as to washing or dry cleaning (if you are not going to keep the ball band, make a record of this information in a notebook). Beaded and sequined projects should be handwashed with as much care as it took to create them. There are specialty dry cleaners who can care for beaded or sequined fabrics. When handwashing, use lukewarm water and a suitable detergent, and try not to agitate the item too much. Avoid wringing because this stretches knitted items out of shape and can damage the beads and sequins. Gently squeeze out the excess water by placing the item on a towel and applying light pressure. Felted items, although already shrunk, should be handwashed to avoid additional shrinkage. Avoid hanging heavily beaded items because this could cause them to sag and stretch.

Quick & easy projects

This chapter contains 20 projects that are embellished with beads and sequins. They include items that you can wear, from accessories such as bags, a belt, and jewelry, to garments such as a skirt, shrug, and cape. There are also projects for the home, including pillows, a throw, and scented sachets. Always read the abbreviations listed for each pattern, because there may be special instructions for that particular project.

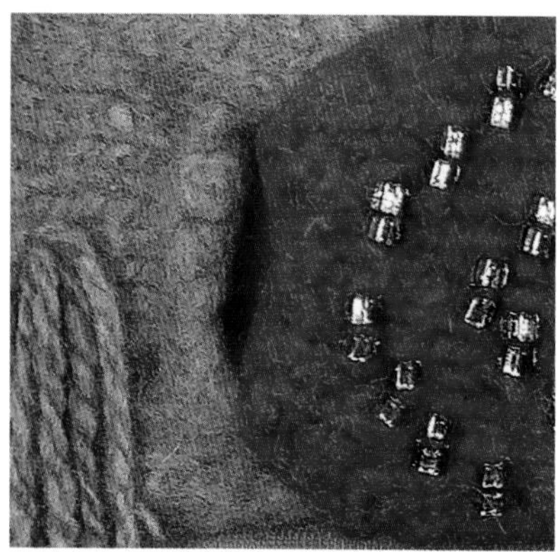

Project 1: Funky felted belt

This simple hipster belt is made up of individually knitted pieces that are felted, linked together in alternating colors, and then finished off with a horn buckle. The darker colored links have beads incorporated during the knitting process, while the lighter colored links are embellished with beaded tassels after knitting, although you could decorate them with buttons or embroidery instead if you prefer.

HEAD LINK

Thread 36 green beads onto yarn A. Using size 9 (5.5 mm) needles and yarn A, cast on 11 sts. Beginning at the bottom right of the chart opposite, work the link, placing the beads and lace hole as indicated. To shape the link, decrease at the beginning of a row by k2tog tbl; decrease at the end of a row by k2tog. When the last row of the chart has been completed, bind off knitwise.

GREEN-BEADED LINKS (make 3)

Thread 36 green beads onto yarn A. Using size 9 (5.5 mm) needles and yarn A, cast on 7 sts.

Row 1 (RS): Knit.

Row 2: K1, m1, purl to last st, m1, k1 (9 sts).

Row 3: K1, m1, knit to last st, m1, k1 (11 sts).

Row 4: K1, purl to last st, k1.

Row 5: K1, m1, knit to last st, m1, k1 (13 sts).

Row 6: K1, purl to last st, k1.

Row 7: K3, bind off next 7 sts knitwise. Slip remaining loop from right to left needle and use cable method to cast on 8 sts. Knit these 8 sts, then knit to end (14 sts).

Row 8: K1, p9, p2tog, p1, k1 (13 sts).

Continue working from the basic link chart below, beginning at the bottom right, and shaping the link and placing beads as indicated. Work the decreases as instructed for the head link. When the last row of the chart has been completed, bind off knitwise.

Basic link

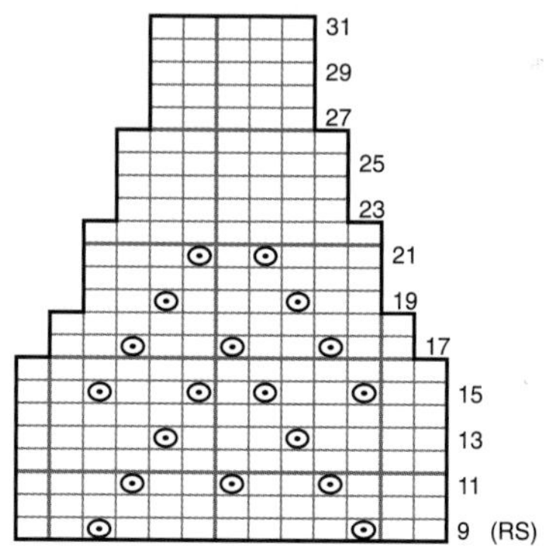

KEY (all charts)

- k on RS, p on WS
- p on RS, k on WS
- k2tog
- yo
- m1
- bead 2

before you start

MEASUREMENTS

2½" (6 cm) wide x 34–38" (86–96 cm) long excluding tail

YARN

DK-weight yarn (100% pure new wool; approx. 123 yds/113 m per 2 oz/50 g ball) in 2 colors:

A Red x 1 ball

B Pink x 1 ball

BEADS AND NOTIONS

180 x 3 mm green beads

144 x 3 mm blue beads

80 x 3 mm orange beads

80 x 3 mm silver beads

2 x 2½" (4.5 x 6 cm) horn buckle

NEEDLES

Size 9 (5.5 mm)

GAUGE

17 sts x 23 rows = 4" (10 cm) in stockinette stitch using size 9 (5.5 mm) needles before felting; 18 sts x 30 rows = 4" (10 cm) after felting

ABBREVIATIONS

bead 2—place 2 beads and slip 1 stitch purlwise; k—knit; m1—make 1 stitch by picking up horizontal bar before next stitch and knitting into back of it; p—purl; RS—right side; st(s)—stitch(es); tbl—through back of loop; tog—together; WS—wrong side; yo—yarn over

Tail link

Head link

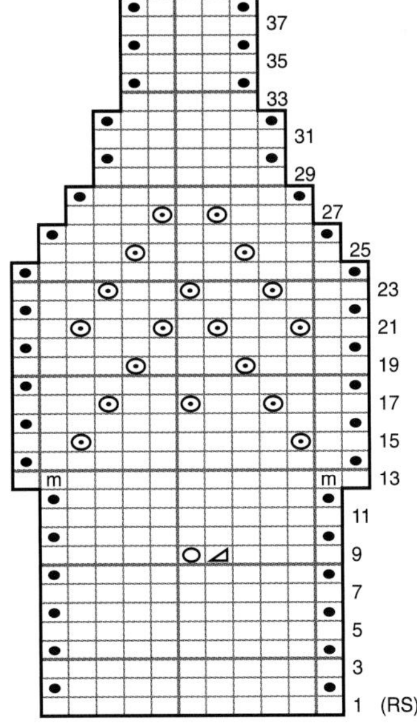

New skills/tassels

Tassels are easy to make and are very effective embellishments.

1 Wrap some yarn around a piece of cardboard that is the length of the tassel you want to make. Vary the number of wraps depending on how thick you want the tassel to be, or as indicated in the pattern.

2 Thread a piece of yarn through the top of the tassel between the yarn and the cardboard. Knot tightly to secure, leaving a long end for sewing the tassel in place.

3 Cut the yarn along the bottom edge of the cardboard. The tassel can be left like this, as in this project. Wrap the long end of yarn around it one or two more times and knot securely.

4 Alternatively, wrap a new length of yarn around the tassel near the top, knot tightly, then repeat one or two times. Trim the tassel.

BLUE-BEADED LINKS (make 4)
Thread 36 blue beads onto yarn A. Using size 9 (5.5 mm) needles and yarn A, cast on 7 sts and continue as for the green-beaded links from row 1 to end.

PLAIN LINKS (make 8)
Using size 9 (5.5 mm) needles and yarn B, cast on 7 sts.
Row 1 (RS): Knit.
Row 2: K1, m1, purl to last st, m1, k1 (9 sts).
Row 3: K1, m1, knit to last st, m1, k1 (11 sts).
Row 4: K1, purl to last st, k1.
Row 5: K1, m1, knit to last st, m1, k1 (13 sts).
Row 6: K1, purl to last st, k1.
Row 7: K3, bind off next 7 sts knitwise. Slip remaining loop from right to left needle, then cast on 8 sts. Knit these 8 sts, then knit to end (14 sts).
Row 8: K1, p10, p2tog, k1 (13 sts).
Row 9: Knit.
Row 10: K1, purl to last st, k1.
Rows 11–16: Repeat rows 9–10 three times.
Row 17: K2tog tbl, knit to last 2 sts, k2tog (11 sts).
Row 18: K1, purl to last st, k1.
Row 19: K2tog tbl, knit to last 2 sts, k2tog (9 sts).
Row 20: K1, purl to last st, k1.
Row 21: Knit.
Row 22: K1, purl to last st, k1.
Row 23: K2tog tbl, knit to last 2 sts, k2tog (7 sts).
Row 24: K1, purl to last st, k1.
Row 25: Knit.
Row 26: K1, purl to last st, k1.
Rows 27–30: Repeat rows 23–26 once.
Bind off knitwise.

TAIL LINK
Thread 36 green beads onto yarn A. Using size 9 (5.5 mm) needles and yarn A, cast on 7 sts. Work rows 1–8 as for the green-beaded links. Continue working from the tail link chart on page 43, beginning at the bottom right of the chart, and shaping the link and placing beads as indicated.

Work the decreases as instructed for the head link. When the last row of the chart has been completed, bind off knitwise.

FINISHING
Weave in any loose ends. Thread a piece of scrap cotton yarn through the corners of all the links and tie together loosely; this will keep them all together during the felting process. Felt and allow to dry thoroughly, then block and steam gently. Start joining the pieces together by inserting the narrow end of the head link through the opening of a plain link from RS to WS. Fold back the narrow end by 1" (2.5 cm) and sew in place to the WS of plain link. To make the links really secure, you need to sew the narrow end to the WS of the plain link around all three edges, then sew the plain link to the WS of the head link where they touch. Use the same technique to link the remaining pieces together, alternating green- and blue-beaded links, with a plain

link between each pair of beaded links. Use yarn A when sewing a plain link to a beaded link, and yarn B when sewing a beaded link to a plain link. Sew the narrow end of the last plain link through the opening in the tail link. Place the pin of the buckle through the lace hole in the head link, then fold back the end of the link and sew securely to hold the buckle in place. Using yarn B, make eight 4" (10 cm) long tassels using five wraps around the cardboard. Thread two beads onto the end of each strand of yarn in the tassels, using 10 orange and 10 silver beads per tassel, and knotting them securely in place. Sew a tassel to the center of each plain link.

To make the belt longer or shorter, simply knit more or fewer links. Each link is 2–2¼" (5–6 cm) long; remember to alternate the colors of the links.

New skills/felting

This is a process of shrinking a woolen fabric by washing it in soapy water to bind the fibers together to create a more solid and fluffy fabric. Felting will not work with superwash wools, cottons, or synthetic yarns. It can be done by hand but is easier in a washing machine.

Felting is very much a case of trial and error, because the water temperature and agitation strength of each washing machine varies. Too cool a wash for too short a time and the fabric will not shrink enough; too hot a wash for too long and your knitting could resemble concrete. It is therefore a good idea to felt the gauge test swatch first, remembering to work a couple of extra stitches and rows to allow for the fabric edges rolling and to make measuring more accurate.

Wash the piece at 100°F (40°C) on your machine's quick or half-wash program (approx. 30–40 minute long) using about ½ cup of a detergent suitable for wool use. Putting a towel into the wash will contribute to the felting process. When the wash cycle is complete, ease the damp swatch into shape by patting, pulling, and smoothing as necessary. Allow to air dry and then measure the swatch.

If the swatch is smaller than the specified gauge in the pattern, the piece has felted too much, so shorten the wash cycle. If it is larger, wash for a bit longer. It is important that you keep notes of all details while you experiment so that you can repeat it successfully with the finished project.

Project 2: Slanted sequined scarf

This scarf literally gives a new twist to the standard stripy scarf. The shape is achieved by increasing and decreasing at the ends of every other row. Knitted in a beautifully soft merino wool/cashmere blend yarn and embellished with sequins in two colors, it will look great for both day and evening wear.

before you start

MEASUREMENTS
8" (20 cm) wide x 61½" (156 cm) long

YARN
DK-weight yarn (57% merino wool, 33% microfiber, 10% cashmere; approx. 142 yds/130 m per 2 oz/50 g ball) in 5 colors:
A Cream x 3 balls
B Orange x 1 ball
C Pink x 1 ball
D Brown x 1 ball
E Crimson x 1 ball

SEQUINS
258 x 8 mm gold sequins
384 x 8 mm red sequins

NEEDLES
Size 6 (4 mm)

GAUGE
22 sts x 30 rows = 4" (10 cm) in stockinette stitch using size 6 (4 mm) needles

ABBREVIATIONS
k—knit; k1f&b—knit into front and back of stitch; p—purl; RS—right side; seq 1—place 1 sequin and slip 1 stitch purlwise; st(s)—stitches; tog—together; WS—wrong side

MAIN PANEL
Thread 384 red sequins onto yarn A and 258 gold sequins onto yarn E. Using yarn D and size 6 (4 mm) needles, cast on 45 sts. Beginning at the bottom right of the chart on page 48, work the scarf, changing colors and placing sequins as indicated. When the last row of the chart has been completed, repeat rows 7–90 four times, then rows 1–60 once. Bind off knitwise using yarn C.

FINISHING
Weave in any loose ends, then block and steam gently.

New skills

Carrying yarn up side of work, see page 99

Sequins with a holographic coating have been used here. These allow you to choose subtly toning colors that will not overpower the striped design, while still giving the scarf extra sparkle.

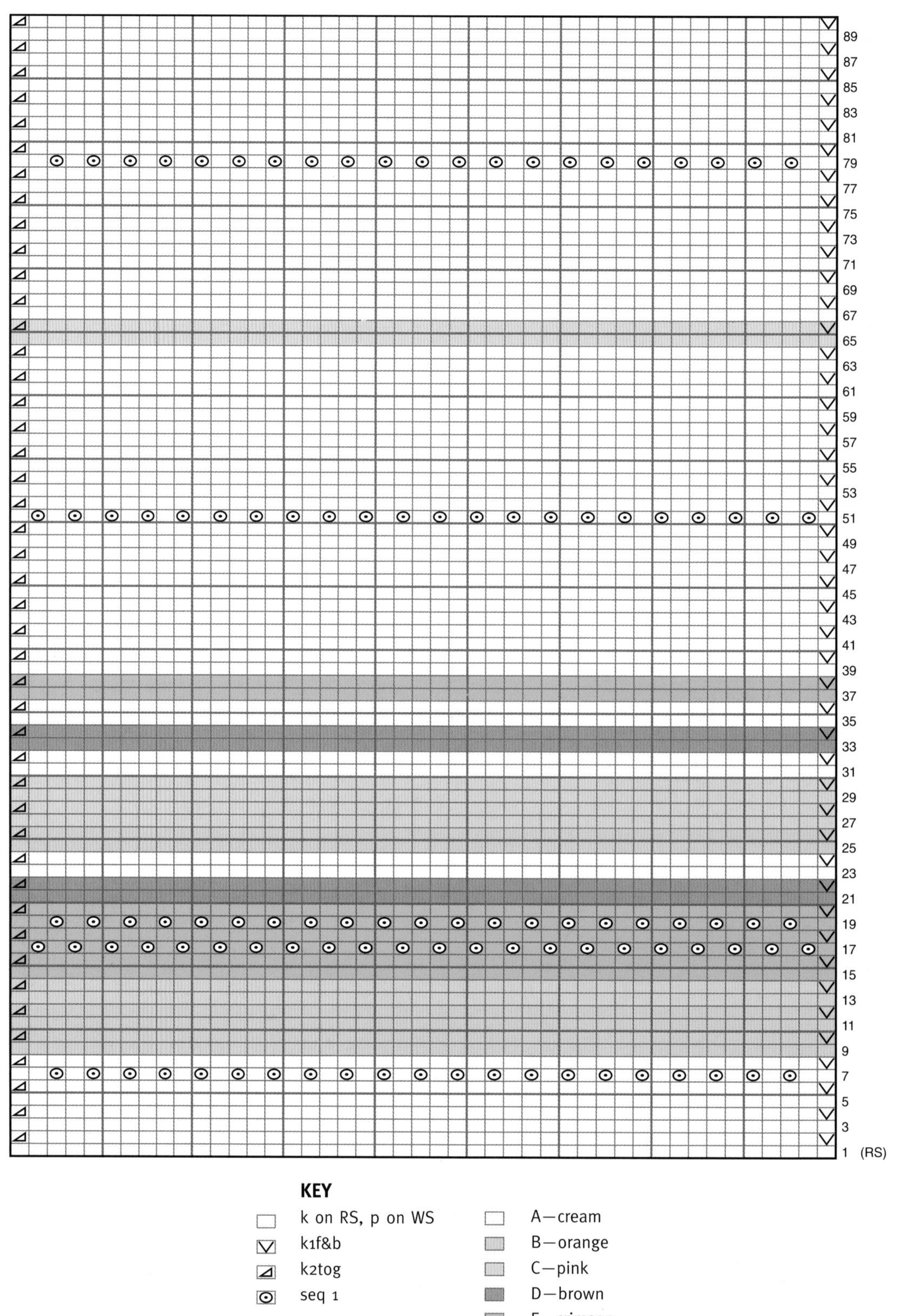
89
87
85
83
81
79
77
75
73
71
69
67
65
63
61
59
57
55
53
51
49
47
45
43
41
39
37
35
33
31
29
27
25
23
21
19
17
15
13
11
9
7
5
3
1 (RS)
KEY
k on RS, p on WS
k1f&b
k2tog
seq 1
A—cream
B—orange
C—pink
D—brown
E—crimson

Project 3: Laced bikini

This pretty "posing" bikini is knitted in a mercerized cotton yarn that gives definition to the stitch pattern, but beware: it will sag if you go for a swim. With its rib pattern and lace-up front and back, the top will fit a number of sizes, but is not really suitable for very large chests. The briefs are graded in three sizes, with a tie fastening at the sides to echo the bikini top. Although worked in sugary pink with bright yellow beads, it would look just as effective knitted in black with white beads for a classic monochrome look.

TOP—RIGHT PANEL

Thread 174 beads onto the yarn. Using size 3 (3.25 mm) needles, cast on 95 sts.

Row 1 (RS): P4, (k1, bead 1) to last 5 sts, k1, p4.

Row 2: K4, purl to last 4 sts, k4.

Row 3: P4, k2, (bead 1, k1) to last 5 sts, k1, p4.

Row 4: K4, purl to last 4 sts, k4.

Row 5: P4, (k5, p3) 5 times, k5, p5, (k5, p3) 4 times, k5, p4.

Row 6: K1, k2tog, yo, k1, p1, k2tog, yo, k1, (p1, k3) 8 times, p1, k5, (p1, k3) to last 9 sts, p1, k2tog, yo, k1, p1, k2tog, yo, k2.

Row 7: As row 5.

Row 8: K4, (p1, k3) 9 times, p1, k5, (p1, k3) to last 5 sts, p1, k4.

Row 9: P4, (k5, p3) 5 times, k5, p1, m1, p3, m1, p1, (k5, p3) 4 times, k5, p4 (97 sts).

Row 10: K4, (p1, k3) 9 times, p1, k7, (p1, k3) to last 5 sts, p1, k4.

Row 11: P4, (k5, p3) 5 times, k5, p7, (k5, p3) 4 times, k5, p4.

Row 12: K1, k2tog, yo, k1, p1, k2tog, yo, k1, (p1, k3) 8 times, p1, k7, (p1, k3) to last 9 sts, p1, k2tog, yo, k1, p1, k2tog, yo, k2.

Row 13: As row 11.

Row 14: As row 10.

Row 15: As row 11.

before you start

MEASUREMENTS

Top Each panel = 13⅜" (34 cm) long x 5" (12.5 cm) wide

Briefs Small [medium, large]

Small = 36–38" (92–96 cm) hips

Medium = 39–41" (100–104 cm) hips

Large = 41–42½" (104–108 cm) hips

YARN

Light-weight yarn (100% cotton; approx. 137 yds/115 m per 2 oz/50 g ball) x 4 balls (pink)

BEADS

679 [691, 703] x 3 mm yellow beads for knitted pieces

96 extra beads for twisted cords

NEEDLES

Size 3 (3.25 mm)

GAUGE

23 sts x 32 rows = 4" (10 cm) in stockinette stitch using size 3 (3.25 mm) needles

ABBREVIATIONS

bead 1—place 1 bead and slip 1 stitch purlwise; k—knit; m1—make 1 stitch by picking up horizontal bar before next stitch and knitting into back of it; p—purl; RS—right side; st(s)—stitch(es); tbl—through back of loop; tog—together; WS—wrong side; yo—yarn over

This pretty bikini has tie fastenings to make it easy to adjust the size to suit your figure. The length of the straps can also be altered, but remember that longer straps will require more beads.

Row 16: As row 10.
Row 17: P4, (k5, p3) 5 times, k5, p1, m1, p5, m1, p1, (k5, p3) 4 times, k5, p4 (99 sts).
Row 18: K1, k2tog, yo, k1, p1, k2tog, yo, k1, (p1, k3) 8 times, p1, k9, (p1, k3) to last 9 sts, p1, k2tog, yo, k1, p1, k2tog, yo, k2.
Row 19: P4, (k5, p3) 5 times, k5, p9, (k5, p3) 4 times, k5, p4.
Row 20: K4, (p1, k3) 9 times, p1, k9, (p1, k3) to last 5 sts, p1, k4.
Row 21: As row 19.
Row 22: As row 20.
Row 23: As row 19.
Row 24: As row 18.
Row 25: P4, (k5, p3) 5 times, k5, p1, m1, p7, m1, p1, (k5, p3) 4 times, k5, p4 (101 sts).
Row 26: K4, (p1, k3) 9 times, p1, k11, (p1, k3) to last 5 sts, p1, k4.
Row 27: P4, (k5, p3) 5 times, k5, p11, (k5, p3) 4 times, k5, p4.
Rows 28–29: Repeat rows 26–27 once.
Row 30: K1, k2tog, yo, k1, p1, k2tog, yo, k1, (p1, k3) 8 times, p1, k11, (p1, k3) to last 9 sts, p1, k2tog, yo, k1, p1, k2tog, yo, k2.
Row 31: As row 27.
Row 32: As row 26.
Row 33: As row 27.
Row 34: As row 26.
Row 35: As row 27.
Row 36: As row 30.
Rows 37–42: Repeat rows 31–35 once.
Row 43: P4, (k5, p3) 5 times, k5, p2tog, p7, p2tog tbl, (k5, p3) 4 times, k5, p4 (99 sts).
Row 44: As row 20.
Row 45: As row 19.
Row 46: As row 20.
Row 47: As row 19.
Row 48: As row 30.
Row 49: P4, k1, (bead 1, k1) to last 5 sts, k1, p4.
Row 50: K4, purl to last 4 sts, k4.
Row 51: P4, k2, (bead 1, k1) to last 5 sts, k1, p4.
Bind off knitwise.

New skills/twisted cord

Twisted cords are a simple way of creating a sturdy drawstring. You can use the same yarn as the rest of the project, or turn it into a design detail by making it in a contrasting color. Twisted cords can be made by twisting together any number of strands; each strand should be about two-and-a-half times the desired finished length of the cord.

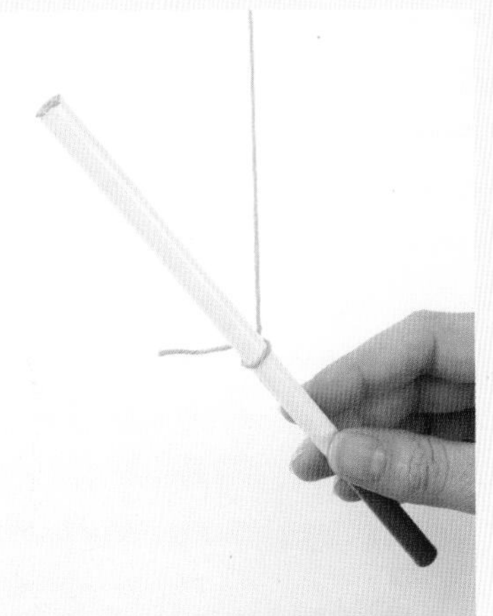

1 Measure out the required length (or lengths) of yarn. Secure one end to a door handle or similar anchor. Holding the free end of the yarn, stand far enough away from the anchor so that the yarn does not droop. Tie the yarn around a pencil. Twist the pencil and yarn around in one direction until it is tight, and the twisted yarn wants to curl back on itself. It is important to get plenty of twist into the yarn.

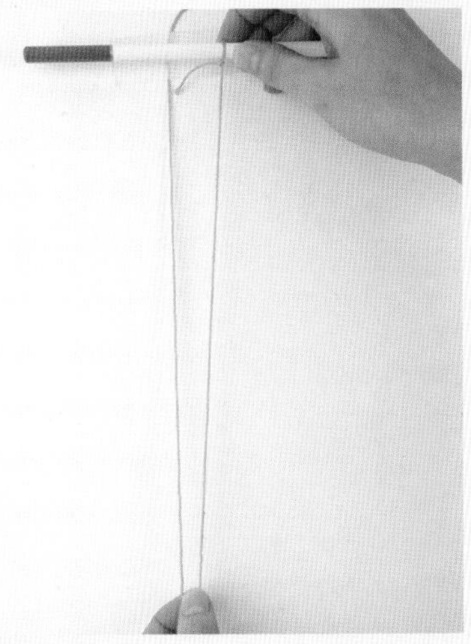

2 Holding the pencil firmly in one hand, pinch the middle of the yarn with the thumb and forefinger of your other hand. Take the pencil up to the anchor and let go of the middle of the yarn. If the cord is too long for you to do this yourself, ask a friend to help. The yarn will twist itself into a cord; if it seems too slack, more twisting is needed.

3 Knot the ends together to prevent the cord from untwisting, and smooth out any bumps using your fingers. Cut the folded end of the cord to separate the strands of yarn. Thread beads onto each strand if instructed, knotting them securely in place.

TOP—LEFT PANEL

Thread 174 beads onto the yarn. Using size 3 (3.25 mm) needles, cast on 95 sts.

Row 1 (RS): P4, (k1, bead 1) to last 5 sts, k1, p4.

Row 2: K4, purl to last 4 sts, k4.

Row 3: P4, k2, (bead 1, k1) to last 5 sts, k1, p4.

Row 4: K4, purl to last 4 sts, k4.

Row 5: P4, (k5, p3) 4 times, k5, p5, (k5, p3) 5 times, k5, p4.

Row 6: K1, k2tog, yo, k1, p1, k2tog, yo, k1, (p1, k3) 10 times, p1, k5, (p1, k3) to last 9 sts, p1, k2tog, yo, k1, p1, k2tog, yo, k2.

Row 7: As row 5.

Row 8: K4, (p1, k3) 11 times, p1, k5, (p1, k3) to last 5 sts, p1, k4.

Row 9: P4, (k5, p3) 4 times, k5, p1, m1, p3, m1, p1, (k5, p3) 5 times, k5, p4 (97 sts).

Row 10: K4, (p1, k3) 11 times, p1, k7, (p1, k3) to last 5 sts, p1, k4.

Row 11: P4, (k5, p3) 4 times, k5, p7, (k5, p3) 5 times, k5, p4.

Row 12: K1, k2tog, yo, k1, p1, k2tog, yo, k1, (p1, k3) 10 times, p1, k7, (p1, k3) to last 9 sts, p1, k2tog, yo, k1, p1, k2tog, yo, k2.

Row 13: As row 11.

Row 14: As row 10.

Row 15: As row 11.

Row 16: As row 10.

Row 17: P4, (k5, p3) 4 times, k5, p1, m1, p5, m1, p1, (k5, p3) 5 times, k5, p4 (99 sts).

Row 18: K1, k2tog, yo, k1, p1, k2tog, yo, k1, (p1, k3) 10 times, p1, k9, (p1, k3) to last 9 sts, p1, k2tog, yo, k1, p1, k2tog, yo, k2.

Row 19: P4, (k5, p3) 4 times, k5, p9, (k5, p3) 5 times, k5, p4.

Row 20: K4, (p1, k3) 11 times, p1, k9, (p1, k3) to last 5 sts, p1, k4.

Row 21: As row 19.

Row 22: As row 20.

Row 23: As row 19.

Row 24: As row 18.

Row 25: P4, (k5, p3) 4 times, k5, p1, m1, p7, m1, p1, (k5, p3) 5 times, k5, p4 (101 sts).

Row 26: K4, (p1, k3) 11 times, p1, k11, (p1, k3) to last 5 sts, p1, k4.

Row 27: P4, (k5, p3) 4 times, k5, p11, (k5, p3) 5 times, k5, p4.

Rows 28–29: Repeat rows 26–27 once.

Row 30: K1, k2tog, yo, k1, p1, k2tog, yo, k1, (p1, k3) 10 times, p1, k11, (p1, k3) to last 9 sts, p1, k2tog, yo, k1, p1, k2tog, yo, k2.

Row 31: As row 27.

Row 32: As row 26.

Row 33: As row 27.

Row 34: As row 26.

Row 35: As row 27.

Row 36: As row 30.

Rows 37–42: Repeat rows 31–35 once.

Row 43: P4, (k5, p3) 4 times, k5, p2tog, p7, p2tog tbl, (k5, p3) 5 times, k5, p4 (99 sts).

Row 44: As row 20.

Row 45: As row 19.

Row 46: As row 20.

Row 47: As row 19.

Row 48: As row 30.

Row 49: P4, k1, (bead 1, k1) to last 5 sts, k1, p4.

Row 50: K4, purl to last 4 sts, k4.

Row 51: P4, k2, (bead 1, k1) to last 5 sts, k1, p4.

Bind off knitwise.

NOTE: Adjusting the straps

Beading will give some elasticity in the strap. To find your strap length, measure over your shoulder to 1" (2.5 cm) below your armhole, back and front. The pattern instructions will fit 17–20" (43–51 cm). If you have to make an adjustment, add or deduct 6 sts and beads for each 1" (2.5 cm).

STRAPS (make 2)

Check the length of strap you need to make (see box, left). Thread 104 beads onto the yarn. Using size 3 (3.25 mm) needles, cast on 115 sts.

Row 1 (RS): P5, (k1, bead 1) to last 7 sts, k2, p5.

Row 2: K5, purl to last 5 sts, k5.

Row 3: P5, k2, (bead 1, k1) to last 5 sts, p5.

Row 4: K5, purl to last 5 sts, k5.

Row 5 (fold line): Purl.

Row 6: K5, purl to last 5 sts, k5.

Row 7: P5, knit to last 5 sts, p5.

Row 8: K5, purl to last 5 sts, k5.

Rows 9–10: Repeat rows 7–8 once.

Bind off knitwise.

SMALL BRIEFS—BACK PIECE

Thread 89 beads onto the yarn. Using size 3 (3.25 mm) needles, cast on 109 sts.

Row 1 (RS): P4, k1, p4, k2, (bead 1, k1) to last 10 sts, (k1, p4) twice.

Row 2: K1, k2tog, yo, k1, p1, k1, yo, k2tog, k1, purl to last 9 sts, k1, k2tog, yo, k1, p1, k1, yo, k2tog, k1.

Row 3: P4, k1, p4, (k1, bead 1) to last 10 sts, (k1, p4) twice.

Row 4: K4, p1, k4, purl to last 9 sts, k4, p1, k4.

Row 5: Bind off 16 sts knitwise at beginning of row, knit to last 9 sts, p4, k1, p4 (93 sts).

Row 6: Bind off 16 sts knitwise at beginning of row, purl to last 2 sts, k2 (77 sts).

Row 7: K2tog, knit to last 2 sts, k2tog (75 sts).

Row 8: K2, purl to last 2 sts, k2.

Repeat rows 7–8 until 13 sts remain, ending with RS facing. Break off yarn and leave sts on a stitch holder.

SMALL BRIEFS—FRONT PIECE

Thread 59 beads onto the yarn. Using size 3 (3.25 mm) needles, cast on 79 sts.

Row 1 (RS): P4, k1, p4, (k1, bead 1) to last 10 sts, (k1, p4) twice.

Row 2: K1, k2tog, yo, k1, p1, k1, yo, k2tog, k1, purl to last 9 sts, k1, k2tog, yo, k1, p1, k1, yo, k2tog, k1.

Row 3: (P4, k1) twice, (k1, bead 1) to last 11 sts, k2, p4, k1, p4.

Row 4: K4, p1, k4, purl to last 9 sts, k4, p1, k4.

Row 5: Bind off 13 sts knitwise at beginning of row, knit to last 9 sts, p4, k1, p4 (66 sts).
Row 6: Bind off 13 sts knitwise at beginning of row, purl to last 2 sts, k2 (53 sts).
****Row 7:** Knit.
Row 8: K2tog, k1, purl to last 3 sts, k1, k2tog.
Row 9: Knit.
Row 10: K2, purl to last 2 sts, k2.
Row 11: K2tog, knit to last 2 sts, k2tog.
Row 12: K2, purl to last 2 sts, k2.
Repeat rows 7–12 until 13 sts remain**. Continue working in stockinette stitch, keeping edge sts as set above, until crotch measures 4" (10 cm), ending with RS facing.

MEDIUM BRIEFS—BACK PIECE

Thread 95 beads onto the yarn. Using size 3 (3.25 mm) needles, cast on 115 sts. Work as for first 6 rows of small size.
Row 7: K2tog, knit to last 2 sts, k2tog.
Row 8: K2, purl to last 2 sts, k2.
Repeat rows 7–8 until 13 sts remain, ending with RS facing. Break off yarn and leave sts on a stitch holder.

MEDIUM BRIEFS—FRONT PIECE

Thread 65 beads onto the yarn. Using size 3 (3.25 mm) needles, cast on 85 sts. Work as for first 6 rows of small size.
Row 7: K2tog, knit to last 2 sts, k2tog.
Row 8: K2, purl to last 2 sts, k2.
Repeat rows 7–8 twice, then work as for small size from ** to **. Continue working in stockinette stitch, keeping edge sts as set above, until crotch measure 4⅜" (11 cm), ending with RS facing.

LARGE BRIEFS—BACK PIECE

Thread 101 beads onto the yarn. Using size 3 (3.25 mm) needles, cast on 121 sts. Work as for first 6 rows of small size.
Row 7: K2tog, knit to last 2 sts, k2tog.
Row 8: K2, purl to last 2 sts, k2.
Repeat rows 7–8 until 13 sts remain, ending with RS facing. Break off yarn and leave sts on a stitch holder.

LARGE BRIEFS—FRONT PIECE

Thread 71 beads onto the yarn. Using size 3 (3.25 mm) needles, cast on 91 sts. Work as for first 6 rows of small size.
Row 7: K2tog, knit to last 2 sts, k2tog.
Row 8: K2, purl to last 2 sts, k2.
Repeat rows 7–8 five times, then work as for small size from ** to **. Continue working in stockinette stitch, keeping edge sts as set above, until crotch measures 4½" (11.5 cm), ending with RS facing.

FINISHING THE TOP

Weave in any loose ends, then block and steam gently. Fold the straps along the fold line WS together and sew cast-on and bind-off edges together. On the right panel, fold the first 4 sts inward at both edges so that the lace holes are matched, then sew in place on WS. On the bind-off edge, position a marker 2½" (6 cm) in from the fold at the right edge, and another marker 2¾" (7 cm) in from the fold at the left edge. Sew the strap in place at the markers, ¾" (2 cm) below the bind-off edge. On the left panel, fold the first 4 sts inward at both edges so that the lace holes are matched, then sew in place on WS. On the bind-off edge, position a marker 2¾" (7 cm) in from the fold at the right edge and another marker 2½" (6 cm) in from the fold at the left edge. Sew the strap in place as before.

Make two twisted cords, one 3' (100 cm) long and the other 5' (150 cm) long, using a single strand of yarn to make each one. Tie a knot approximately 1½" (4 cm) from each end of both cords, cut the folded end, and thread 6 beads onto each strand of yarn at both ends of each cord. Knot to secure the beads in place. Lace the bikini top together at the back by threading the shorter cord through the lace holes, beginning at the top edge and ending at the bind-off edge. Tie the cord into a bow. Use the longer cord to lace the top together at the front in the same way.

FINISHING THE BRIEFS

Holding the front and back pieces RS together in your left hand, bind off both sets of sts together. Weave in any loose ends, then block and steam gently. Fold under the first 4 sts at the side waist on the front piece so that the lace holes match, then sew in place on WS. Repeat on the other side of the front piece and on both sides of the back piece. Make two 4' (120 cm) long twisted cords and finish the ends with beads as before. Thread a cord through the lace holes at each side of the briefs to fasten them.

Project 4: Beaded float choker and bracelet

This jewelry set is perfect for any occasion, dressed up with a classic black cocktail gown, or dressed down with jeans for a casual look. The sport-weight cotton yarn has a mercerized finish that contrasts with the frosted beads. Matching beaded buttons complete the look.

CHOKER

Thread 228 [240] beads onto the yarn. Using size 2 (2.75 mm) needles, cast on 103 [113] sts.

Row 1 (WS): (K1, p1) to last st, k1.

Row 2 (RS): K6 [11], bead 7, (k7, bead 7) to last 6 [11] sts, k6 [11].

Row 3: Purl.

Row 4: K2 [7], *bead 1, k4, bead 5, k4, repeat from * to last 3 [8] sts, bead 1, k2 [7].

Row 5: Purl.

Row 6: K2 [6], bead 2 [3], (k4, bead 3), to last 8 [13] sts, k4, bead 2 [3], k2 [6].

Row 7: Purl.

Row 8: K2 [5], bead 3 [5], k4, bead 1, k4, bead 5, repeat from * to last 14 [19] sts, k4, bead 1, k4, bead 3 [5], k2 [5].

Row 9: Purl.

Row 10: K2 [4], bead 4 [7], k7, (bead 7, k7) to last 6 [11] sts, bead 4 [7], k2 [4].

Row 11: Purl.

Row 12: (K1, p1) to last st, k1.

Bind off in k1, p1 pattern.

BRACELET

Thread 79 beads onto the yarn. Using size 2 (2.75 mm) needles, cast on 59 [63] sts.

Row 1 (WS): (K1, p1) to last st, k1.

Row 2 (RS): K1 [3], bead 4, k7, (bead 7, k7) to last 5 [7] sts, bead 4, k1 [3].

Row 3: Purl.

Row 4: K1 [3], bead 3, k4, *bead 1, k4, bead 5, k4, repeat from * to last 9 [11] sts, bead 1, k4, bead 3, k1 [3].

Row 5: Purl.

Row 6: K1 [3], bead 2, K4, (bead 3, k4) to last 3 [5] sts, bead 2, k1 [3].

Row 7: Purl.

Row 8: K1 [3], bead 1, *k4, bead 5, k4, bead 1, repeat from * to last 6 [8] sts, k4, bead 1, k1 [3].

Row 9: Purl.

Row 10: K5 [7], (bead 7, k7) to last 12 [14] sts, bead 7, k5 [7].

Row 11: Purl.

Row 12: (K1, p1) to last st, k1.

Bind off in k1, p1 pattern.

BEADED BUTTONS (make 2)

Thread 9 beads onto the yarn. Using size 2 (2.75 mm) needles, cast on 3 sts.

Row 1 (RS): K1, bead 1, k1.

Row 2: P1f&b, purl to last st, p1f&b (5 sts).

Row 3: (K1, bead 1) twice, k1.

Row 4: P1f&b, purl to last st, p1f&b (7 sts).

Row 5: (K1, bead 1) 3 times, k1.

Row 6: P2tog, purl to last st, p2tog (5 sts).

before you start

MEASUREMENTS

Choker Small [large]
Small = 1" (2.5 cm) wide x 12½" (32 cm) long
Large = 1" (2.5 cm) wide x 14" (36 cm) long

Bracelet Small [large]
Small = 1" (2.5 cm) wide x 7¼" (18.5 cm) long
Large = 1" (2.5 cm) wide x 7¾" (19.5 cm) long

YARN

Sport-weight yarn (100% cotton; approx. 153 yds/140 m per 2 oz/50 g ball) x 1 ball (blue)

BEADS AND NOTIONS

370 [380] x 3 mm green beads
27" (70 cm) length of 1" (2.5 cm) wide blue ribbon

NEEDLES

Size 2 (2.75 mm)

GAUGE

32 sts x 46 rows = 4" (10 cm) in stockinette stitch using size 2 (2.75 mm) needles

ABBREVIATIONS

bead—place specified number of beads and slip same number of stitches purlwise; k—knit; p—purl; p1f&b—purl into front and back of stitch; RS—right side; st(s)—stitch(es); tog—together; WS—wrong side

Row 7: (K1, bead 1) twice, k1.
Row 8: P2tog, p1, p2tog.
Row 9: K1, bead 1, k1.
Row 10: P3tog.
Fasten off, leaving a long end of yarn.

Vivid blue and green were chosen to make these striking pieces of jewelry, but you could choose pastel colors for a summery look, or black and gold for evening wear.

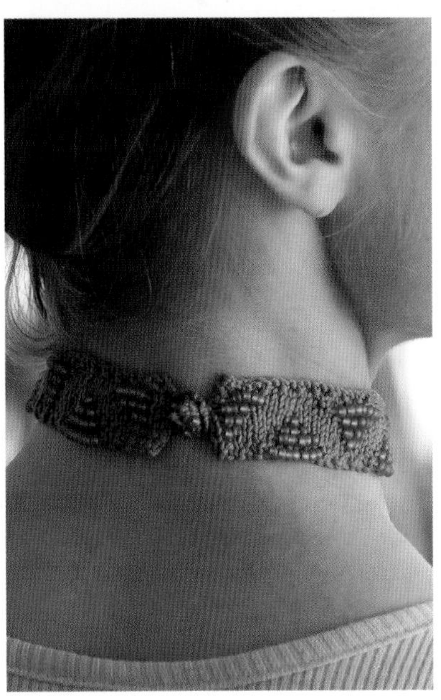

FINISHING

Thread a needle with the long end of yarn on a beaded button, then fold the edges of the button toward the center, WS together. Run the yarn through the edge sts and pull up as tightly as possible to make a button shape. Fasten off, leaving another long end of yarn to sew the button in place. Weave in any loose ends. In the center of one side edge of the choker, make a loop fastening large enough to pass the button through. Sew the button to the opposite side of the choker. Cut the ribbon approximately 1½" (4 cm) longer than the choker and sew it to the WS of the knitted piece using matching colored sewing thread and folding under the raw ends of ribbon as you sew. Repeat to complete the bracelet.

New skills

Loop fastenings, see page 58

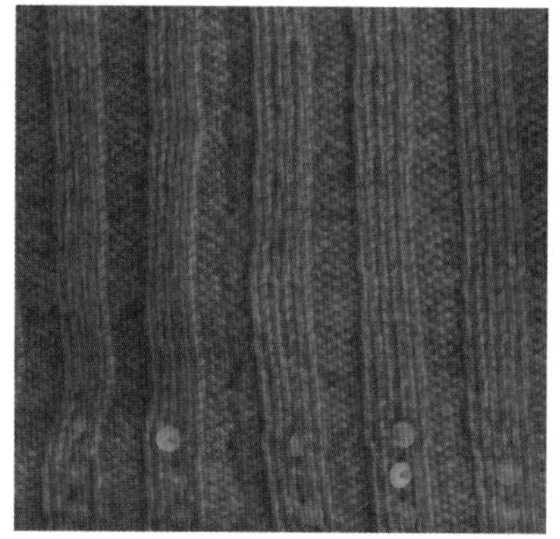

Project 5: Snuggly collar and cuffs

These collar and cuffs are perfect for day or evening wear, and will help you keep warm without covering up your outfit completely. Embellished with clear sequins that subtly catch the light, both collar and cuffs are knitted in cotton/microfiber and kid mohair/silk blend yarns for luxurious softness.

COLLAR PANELS (make 2)

Thread 60 [68, 76] sequins onto yarn A. Using size 8 (5 mm) needles and one end each of yarns A and B, cast on 93 [105, 117] sts.

Row 1 (RS): (P3, k1, seq 1, k1) to last 3 sts, p3.

Row 2: (K3, p3) to last 3 sts, k3.

Row 3: (P3, k3) to last 3 sts, p3.

Row 4: (K3, p3) to last 3 sts, k3.

Rows 5–16: Work in sequined rib as set by rows 1–4.

Row 17: (P3, k3) to last 3 sts, p3.

Row 18: (K3, p3) to last 3 sts, k3.

Work in rib as set by rows 17–18 until collar measures 8¼" (21 cm) from cast-on edge, ending with RS facing for next row. Change to size 7 (4.5 mm) needles and continue in rib for another 8¼" (21 cm). Bind off in rib.

FINISHING

Weave in any loose ends. With RS facing, join the side seams of the collar pieces together using mattress stitch.

CUFFS (make 2)

Using size 7 (4.5 mm) needles and one end each of yarns A and B, cast on 67 sts.

Row 1 (RS): P2, (k3, p3) to last 5 sts, k3, p2.

Row 2: K2, (p3, k3) to last 5 sts, p3, k2.

Rows 3–20: Repeat rows 1–2 nine times.

Change to size 8 (5 mm) needles.

Rows 21–32: Work in rib as set by rows 1–2.

Row 33: P2tog, (k3, p3) to last 5 sts, k3, p2tog (65 sts).

Row 34: K1, (p3, k3) to last 4 sts, p3, k1.

Row 35: P1, (k3, p3) to last 4 sts, k3, p1.

Rows 36–44: Repeat rows 34–35 four times, then row 34 once.

Row 45: K2tog, k2, (p3, k3) to last 7 sts, p3, k2, k2tog (63 sts).

Row 46: (P3, k3) to last 3 sts, p3.

Row 47: (K3, p3) to last 3 sts, k3.

Rows 48–56: Repeat rows 46–47 four times, then row 46 once.

Row 57: K2tog, k1, (p3, k3) to last 6 sts, p3, k1, k2tog (61 sts).

Row 58: P2, (k3, p3) to last 5 sts, k3, p2.

Row 59: K2, (p3, k3) to last 5 sts, p3, k2.

Rows 60–68: Repeat rows 58–59 four times, then row 58 once.

Row 69: K2tog, (p3, k3) to last 5 sts, p3, k2tog (59 sts).

Row 70: P1, (k3, p3) to last 4 sts, k3, p1.

These sequined collar and cuffs in vivid pink make a bold statement. Team them with funky streetwear to attract attention, or use them to keep warm when you go out for an evening in a sleeveless dress or top.

before you start

MEASUREMENTS

Collar Small [medium, large]
Small = 34–36" (88–91 cm) bust
Medium = 36–38" (91–96 cm) bust
Large = 38–40" (96–102 cm) bust
Cuffs One size to fit average-sized adult arms, measuring 19" (48 cm) from top to point of finger

YARN

A DK-weight yarn (75% cotton, 25% microfiber; approx. 175 yds/160 m per 2 oz/50 g ball) x 6 balls (pink)
B Light-weight yarn (70% kid mohair, 30% silk; approx. 229 yds/210 m per 1 oz/25 g ball) x 3 balls (purple)
Yarns A and B are used together throughout

SEQUINS

172 [208, 224] x 8 mm clear sequins

NEEDLES

Size 7 (4.5 mm); size 8 (5 mm)

GAUGE

21 sts x 30 rows = 4" (10 cm) in stockinette stitch using size 8 (5 mm) needles and yarns A and B together

ABBREVIATIONS

k—knit; p—purl; RS—right side; seq 1—place 1 sequin and slip 1 stitch purlwise; st(s)—stitches; tog—together; WS—wrong side

New skills/loop fastenings

This is a very simple but sturdy way of making a fastening device. These are most commonly used for fastening buttons, but can also be used as finger loops.

1 Sew a loop of yarn just big enough to pass the button or finger through, positioning the loop where indicated in the pattern. Make sure that the loop is secure at both ends.

2 Working from one end to the other, reinforce the loop with blanket stitch (see page 65).

Row 71: K1, (p3, k3) to last 4 sts, p3, k1.
Rows 72–80: Repeat rows 70–71 four times, then row 70 once.
Row 81: P2tog, p2, (k3, p3) to last 7 sts, k3, p2, p2tog (57 sts).
Row 82: (K3, p3) to last 3 sts, k3.
Row 83: (P3, k3) to last 3 sts, p3.
Rows 84–96: Repeat rows 82–83 six times, then row 82 once.
Start shaping the hand section of the cuffs as follows.
Row 97: Bind off 11 sts knitwise, rib to end (46 sts).
Row 98: Bind off 11 sts purlwise, rib to end (35 sts).
Row 99: Bind off 7 sts knitwise, rib to end (28 sts).
Row 100: Bind off 8 sts purlwise, rib to last 2 sts, p2tog (19 sts).
Row 101: K2tog, (k3, p3) twice, k3, k2tog (17 sts).
Row 102: P4, k3, p3, k3, p4.
Row 103: K4, p3, k3, p3, k4.
Row 104: P4, k3, p3, k3, p4.
Row 105: K2tog, k2, p3, k3, p3, k2, k2tog (15 sts).
Row 106: (P3, k3) twice, p3.
Row 107: (K3, p3) twice, k3.
Row 108: (P3, k3) twice, p3.
Row 109: K2tog, k1, p3, k3, p3, k1, k2tog (13 sts).
Row 110: P2, k3, p3, k3, p2.
Row 111: K2, p3, k3, p3, k2.
Row 112: P2, k3, p3, k3, p2.
Row 113: K2tog, p3, k3, p3, k2tog (11 sts).
Row 114: P1, k3, p3, k3, p1.
Row 115: K1, p3, k3, p3, k1.
Row 116: P1, k3, p3, k3, p1.
Row 117: K2tog, p2, k3, p2, k2tog (9 sts).
Row 118: P1, k2, p3, k2, p1.
Row 119: K1, p2, k3, p2, k1.
Row 120: K3, p3, k3.
Bind off in rib.

FINISHING

Weave in any loose ends. Starting at the pointed bind-off edge of the cuffs, sew 12 sequins up the central knit stitch of the rib to echo the edge of the collar. Repeat on the ribs either side of the center. Make two loop fastenings large enough to slip your middle finger through at the end of each cuff. Position the first loop at the pointed tip, and the second ¾" (2 cm) below that on the WS. With RS together, sew the center seam using a fine backstitch.

Project 6: Buckled satchel

Inspired by a traditional leather school satchel, this bag combines silk/cotton and wool/cotton blend yarns to create an interesting and unusual tweed effect. The main section of the bag is worked in one piece, making it very simple to knit, with the beading placed on the top flap only.

before you start

MEASUREMENTS
10¼" (26 cm) wide x 10⅝" (27 cm) long excluding handle x 2½" (6 cm) deep

YARN
A Aran-weight yarn (70% silk, 30% cotton; approx. 118 yds/108 m per 2 oz/50 g ball) x 3 balls (red)
B DK-weight yarn (50% wool, 50% cotton; approx. 123 yds/113 m per 2 oz/50 g ball) x 3 balls (orange)
Yarns A and B are used together throughout

BEADS AND NOTIONS
137 x 8 mm wooden beads
2¾" (7 cm) diameter tortoiseshell buckle

NEEDLES
Size 9 (5.5 mm); size 7 (4.5 mm)

GAUGE
15 sts x 20 rows = 4" (10 cm) in stockinette stitch using size 9 (5.5 mm) needles and yarns A and B together

ABBREVIATIONS
bead 1—place 1 bead and slip 1 stitch purlwise; k—knit; p—purl; RS—right side; st(s)—stitch(es); tbl—through back of loop; tog—together; WS—wrong side

MAIN PANEL
Using size 9 (5.5 mm) needles and one end each of yarns A and B, cast on 37 sts.
Row 1 (RS): Knit.
Row 2: K1, purl to last st, k1.
Rows 3–56: Repeat rows 1–2 twenty-seven times.
Row 57 (base fold line): Purl.
Row 58: K1, purl to last st, k1.
Rows 59–68: Repeat rows 1–2 five times.
Row 69 (base fold line): Purl.
Row 70: K1, purl to last st, k1.
Rows 71–123: Repeat rows 1–2 twenty-six times, then repeat row 1 once.
Row 124 (flap fold line): Knit.
Break off both yarns.

BEADED FLAP
Thread 137 beads onto yarn B. Rejoin both yarns to main panel and work flap as follows:
Row 125 (RS): K1, bead 1, k21, bead 1, k11, bead 1, k1.
Row 126 & all unspecified WS rows: K1, purl to last st, k1.
Row 127: K1, bead 1, k20, bead 1, k12, bead 1, k1.
Row 129: K1, bead 1, k17, (bead 1, k1) twice, k13, bead 1, k1.

Large wooden beads have a special tactile appeal. Knitted onto a vivid background of rich oranges and reds, they create an irregular geometric pattern to enhance the flap of the bag.

Row 131: K1, bead 1, k16, (bead 1, k1) twice, k14, bead 1, k1.
Row 133: (K1, bead 1) twice, k13, (bead 1, k1) twice, k12, (bead 1, k1) twice.
Row 135: K1, bead 1, k2, bead 1, k11, (bead 1, k1) 3 times, k10, bead 1, k2, bead 1, k1.
Row 137: K1, bead 1, k3, bead 1, k9, (bead 1, k1) 3 times, k10, bead 1, k3, bead 1, k1.
Row 139: K1, bead 1, k4, bead 1, k7, (bead 1, k1) 3 times, k10, bead 1, k4, bead 1, k1.
Row 140: Knit.
Row 141: K1, (bead 1, k5) twice, (bead 1, k1) 3 times, k10, bead 1, k5, bead 1, k1.
Row 143: K1, bead 1, k6, bead 1, k3, (bead 1, k1) 3 times, k10, bead 1, k6, bead 1, k1.
Row 145: K1, bead 1, k7, (bead 1, k1) 4 times, k10, bead 1, k7, bead 1, k1.
Row 147: K1, bead 1, k8, (bead 1, k1) 3 times, k10, (bead 1, k1) twice, k5, bead 1, k1.
Row 149: K1, bead 1, k9, (bead 1, k1) twice, k10, (bead 1, k1) twice, k6, bead 1, k1.
Row 151: K1, bead 1, k8, (bead 1, k1) twice, k10, (bead 1, k1) twice, k7, bead 1, k1.
Row 153: K1, bead 1, k7, bead 1, k3, bead 1, k9, (bead 1, k1) twice, k8, bead 1, k1.
Row 155: K1, bead 1, k6, bead 1, k5, bead 1, k7, (bead 1, k1) 3 times, k7, bead 1, k1.
Row 157: K1, bead 1, k5, bead 1, k7, bead 1, k5, (bead 1, k1) twice, k2, bead 1, k7, bead 1, k1.
Row 159: K1, bead 1, k4, bead 1, k9, bead 1, k3, (bead 1, k1) twice, k4, bead 1, k6, bead 1, k1.
Row 161: K1, bead 1, k3, bead 1, k11, (bead 1, k1) 3 times, k6, bead 1, k5, bead 1, k1.
Row 163: K2tog tbl, (bead 1, k1) twice, k12, (bead 1, k1) twice, k8, bead 1, k3, bead 1, k2tog (35 sts).
Row 165: K2tog tbl, (bead 1, k1) to last 3 sts, bead 1, k2tog (33 sts).
Row 166: Bind off 12 sts knitwise at beginning of row, purl to last st, k1 (21 sts).
Row 167: Bind off 12 sts knitwise at beginning of row, knit to end (9 sts).
Row 168: K1, purl to last st, k1.
Repeat rows 1–2 until flap measures 3½" (9 cm), ending with RS facing for next row.
Next row (RS): K2tog tbl, knit to last 2 sts, k2tog (7 sts).
Next row: K1, purl to last st, k1.
Repeat these two rows until 3 sts remain, then bind off knitwise.

STRAP

Using size 7 (4.5 mm) needles and one end each of yarns A and B, cast on 9 sts.
Row 1 (RS): Knit.
Row 2: K1, p7, k1.
Repeats rows 1–2 until strap measures 10⅝" (27 cm). Place markers at both ends of last row, then continue repeating rows 1–2 until strap measures 41¾" (106 cm) from first pair of markers. Place a second pair of markers at both ends of last row, then continue repeating rows 1–2 until strap measures 63" (160 cm). Bind off knitwise.

FINISHING

Weave in any loose ends, then block and steam gently. With WS of strap and bag together, align the ends of the strap with the base fold lines on the bag, and align the markers on the strap with the cast-on edge and flap fold line on the bag. Sew the strap in place on the outside of the bag using blanket stitch and yarns A and B together. Position the buckle in the center of the bag front, 5½" (14 cm) below the cast-on edge. Sew the buckle in place using yarns A and B together.

New skills

Blanket stitch, see page 65

Project 7: Slouchy summer bag

This brightly beaded bag is knitted in bulky cotton yarn and would be great for taking on vacation. The beaded fringes made by casting on and then binding off stitches create a lot of texture on the front of the bag, which is contrasted by simple beaded stripes on the back. The handles tie together so that you can adjust the length to suit yourself, wearing the bag over the shoulder or across the body for a casual summer look.

BACK PANEL

Thread 118 beads onto the yarn, alternating 1 white bead and 1 clear bead. Using size 8 (5 mm) needles, cast on 45 sts.

Row 1 (RS): Knit.

Row 2 & all unspecified WS rows: Purl.

Rows 3–8: Beginning with a knit row, work six rows in stockinette stitch.

Row 9: (K1, bead 1) to last st, k1.

Rows 11–14: Beginning with a knit row, work four rows in stockinette stitch.

Row 15: K1, k2tog tbl, knit to last 3 sts, k2tog, k1 (43 sts).

Row 17: (K1, bead 1) to last st, k1.

Rows 19–24: Beginning with a knit row, work six rows in stockinette stitch.

Row 25: K2, (bead 1, k1) to last st, k1.

Row 27: Knit.

Row 29: K1, k2tog tbl, knit to last 3 sts, k2tog, k1 (41 sts).

Row 31: Knit.

Row 33: K2, (bead 1, k1) to last st, k1.

Rows 35–40: Beginning with a knit row, work six rows in stockinette stitch.

Row 41: (K1, bead 1) to last st, k1.

Row 43: K1, k2tog tbl, knit to last 3 sts, k2tog, k1 (39 sts).

Rows 45–48: Beginning with a knit row, work four rows in stockinette stitch.

Row 49: (K1, bead 1) to last st, k1.

Rows 51–56: Beginning with a knit row, work six rows in stockinette stitch.

Row 57: K1, k2tog tbl, knit to last 3 sts, k2tog, k1 (37 sts).

Row 59: Knit.

Rows 60–61: Purl.

Row 62: Knit.

Bind off purlwise.

FRONT PANEL

Thread 254 beads onto the yarn, alternating 1 white bead and 1 clear bead. Using size 8 (5 mm) needles, cast on 45 sts.

Row 1 (RS): Knit.

Row 2 & all unspecified WS rows: Purl.

Row 3: K2, (fringe 1, k3) to last 3 sts, fringe 1, k2.

Row 5: Knit.

Row 7: K4, (fringe 1, k3) to last st, k1.

Row 9: Knit.

Rows 11–14: Repeat rows 3–6.

Row 15: K1, k2tog tbl, k1, (fringe 1, k3) to last 5 sts, fringe 1, k1, k2tog, k1 (43 sts).

Row 17: Knit.

Row 19: K1, (fringe 1, k3) to last 2 sts, fringe 1, k1.

Row 21: Knit.

Row 23: (K3, fringe 1) to last 3 sts, k3.

Row 25: K1, k2tog tbl, knit to last 3 sts, k2tog, k1 (41 sts).

Row 27: K4, (fringe 1, k3) to last st, k1.

Row 29: Knit.

Row 31: K2, (fringe 1, k3) to last 3 sts, fringe 1, k2.

Row 33: Knit.

Row 35: K4, (fringe 1, k3) to last st, k1.

Row 37: K1, k2tog tbl, knit to last 3 sts, k2tog, k1 (39 sts).

Row 39: K1, (fringe 1, k3) to last 2 sts, fringe 1, k1.

before you start

MEASUREMENTS

20½" (52 cm) wide x 29½" (75 cm) long excluding handle

YARN

Bulky-weight yarn (55% cotton, 45% acrylic; approx. 63 yds/58 m per 2 oz/50 g ball) x 10 balls (orange)

BEADS AND NOTIONS

186 x 5 mm white beads
186 x 5 mm clear beads
9" (23 cm) light-weight zipper

NEEDLES

Size 8 (5 mm)

GAUGE

17 sts x 23 rows = 4" (10 cm) in stockinette stitch using size 8 (5 mm) needles

ABBREVIATIONS

bead 1—place 1 bead and slip 1 stitch purlwise; fringe 1—work 1 beaded fringe (see page 36); k—knit; m1—make 1 stitch by picking up horizontal bar before next stitch and working into back of it knitwise on a knit row or purlwise on a purl row; p—purl; RS—right side; st(s)—stitch(es); tbl—through back of loop; tog—together; WS—wrong side

Row 41: Knit.
Row 43: (K3, fringe 1) to last 3 sts, k3.
Row 45: Knit.
Row 47: K1, k2tog tbl, k2, (fringe 1, k3) to last 6 sts, fringe 1, k2, k2tog, k1.
Row 49: Knit.
Row 51: K2, (fringe 1, k3) to last 3 sts, fringe 1, k2.
Row 52: Knit.
Bind off purlwise.

LEFT STRAP (make 2)
Using size 8 (5 mm) needles, cast on 7 sts.
Row 1 (RS): Knit.
Row 2: P1, m1, purl to end (8 sts).
Row 3: Knit to last st, m1, k1 (9 sts).
Rows 4–9: Repeat rows 2–3 three times (15 sts).
Row 10: Purl.
Row 11: Knit to last st, m1, k1 (16 sts).
Row 12: Purl.
Row 13: K1, m1, knit to last st, m1, k1 (18 sts).
Row 14: Purl.
Row 15: Knit to last st, m1, k1 (19 sts).
Rows 16–19: Repeat rows 14–15 twice (21 sts).
Row 20: Purl.
Row 21: Knit.
Row 22: Purl.
Row 23: Knit to last st, m1, k1 (22 sts).
Row 24: Purl.
Row 25: K1, m1, knit to end (23 sts).
Row 26: Purl.
Row 27: Knit to last st, m1, k1 (24 sts).
Row 28: Purl.
Rows 29–32: Beginning with a knit row, work four rows in stockinette stitch.
Row 33: K1, m1, knit to end (25 sts).
Row 34: Purl.
Rows 35–40: Beginning with a knit row, work six rows in stockinette stitch.
Row 41: K1, m1, knit to last 3 sts, k2tog, k1.

Long fringes topped with beads create a highly textured fabric on the front of the bag. The handles are plain, both to highlight the fringing and make the bag comfortable to carry.

Row 42: Purl.
Rows 43–46: Beginning with a knit row, work four rows in stockinette stitch.
Row 47: K1, m1, knit to last 3 sts, k2tog, k1.
Row 48: Purl.
Row 49: Knit.
Row 50: Purl.
Row 51: K1, m1, knit to end (26 sts).
Row 52: Knit.
Row 53: Place marker at beginning of row, then k1, k2tog tbl, knit to last 3 sts, k2tog, k1 (24 sts).
Row 54: Purl.
Row 55: K1, k2tog tbl, knit to end (23 sts).
Row 56: Purl.
Row 57: K1, k2tog tbl, knit to end (22 sts).
Row 58: Purl.
Row 59: As row 53 (20 sts).
Row 60: Purl.
Rows 61–64: Beginning with a knit row, work four rows in stockinette stitch.
Row 65: Knit to last 3 sts, k2tog, k1 (19 sts).
Row 66: Purl.
Rows 67–108: Repeat rows 61–66 seven times (12 sts).
Rows 109–114: Beginning with a knit row, work four rows in stockinette stitch.
Row 115: Knit to last 3 sts, k2tog, k1 (11 sts).
Row 116: Purl.
Rows 117–122: Beginning with a knit row, work six rows in stockinette stitch.
Rows 123–130: Repeat rows 115–122 once (10 sts).
Row 131: Knit to last 3 sts, k2tog, k1 (9 sts).
Row 132: Purl.
Rows 133–140: Beginning with a knit row, work eight rows in stockinette stitch.
Rows 141–180: Repeat rows 131–140 four times.
Bind off remaining 5 sts knitwise.

New skills

Inserting a zipper, see page 70

RIGHT STRAP (make 2)

Using size 8 (5 mm) needles, cast on 7 sts.
Row 1 (RS): Purl.
Row 2: K1, m1, knit to end (8 sts).
Row 3: Purl to last st, m1, p1 (9 sts).
Row 4: K1, m1, knit to end (10 sts).
Row 5: Purl to last st, m1, p1 (11 sts).
Row 6: K1, m1, knit to end (12 sts).
Row 7: Purl to last st, m1, p1 (13 sts).
Row 8: K1, m1, knit to end (14 sts).
Row 9: Purl to last st, m1, p1 (15 sts).
Row 10: Knit.
Row 11: Purl to last st, m1, p1 (16 sts).
Row 12: Knit.
Row 13: P1, m1, purl to last st, m1, p1 (18 sts).
Row 14: Knit.
Row 15: Purl to last st, m1, p1 (19 sts).
Row 16: Knit.
Row 17: Purl to last st, m1, p1 (20 sts).
Row 18: Knit.
Row 19: Purl to last st, m1, p1 (21 sts).
Row 20: Knit.
Row 21: Purl.
Row 22: Knit.
Row 23: Purl to last st, m1, p1 (22 sts).
Row 24: Knit.
Row 25: P1, m1, purl to end (23 sts).
Row 26: Knit.
Row 27: Purl to last st, m1, p1 (24 sts).
Row 28: Knit.
Rows 29–32: Beginning with a purl row, work four rows in stockinette stitch.
Row 33: P1, m1, purl to end (25 sts).
Row 34: Knit.
Rows 35–40: Beginning with a purl row, work six rows in stockinette stitch.
Row 41: P1, m1, purl to last 3 sts, p2tog, p1.
Row 42: Knit.
Rows 43–46: Beginning with a purl row, work four rows in stockinette stitch.
Row 47: P1, m1, purl to last 3 sts, p2tog, p1.
Row 48: Knit.
Row 49: Purl.
Row 50: Knit.
Row 51: P1, m1, purl to end (26 sts).
Row 52: Knit.
Row 53: Place marker at beginning of row, then p1, p2tog, purl to last 3 sts, p2tog tbl, p1 (24 sts).
Row 54: Knit.
Row 55: P1, p2tog, purl to end (23 sts).
Row 56: Knit.
Row 57: P1, p2tog, purl to end (22 sts).
Row 58: Knit.
Row 59: As row 53 (20 sts).
Row 60: Knit.
Rows 61–64: Beginning with a purl row work, four rows in stockinette stitch.
Row 65: Purl to last 3 sts, p2tog tbl, p1 (19 sts).
Row 66: Knit.
Rows 67–108: Repeat rows 61–66 seven times (12 sts).
Rows 109–114: Beginning with a purl row, work four rows in stockinette stitch.
Row 115: Purl to last 3 sts, p2tog, p1 (11 sts).
Row 116: Knit.
Rows 117–122: Beginning with a purl row, work six rows in stockinette stitch.
Rows 123–130: Repeat rows 115–122 once.
Row 131: Purl to last 3 sts, p2tog tbl, p1 (9 sts).
Row 132: Knit.
Rows 133–140: Beginning with a purl row, work eight rows in stockinette stitch.
Rows 141–180: Repeat rows 131–140 four times.
Bind off remaining 5 sts purlwise.

FINISHING

Weave in any loose ends. With RS together, place right strap onto bag front, matching the cast-on edges at the base and the marker on the strap to the top right corner of the bag front. Sew the seam using backstitch, taking care not to trap the fringes. Repeat for the left strap on the opposite side, then repeat for the back of the bag. Position the zipper in the bind-off edges of the middle section of the bag and sew in place with matching sewing thread. Turn the bag WS out so that the RS of all pieces are together and sew the inner seams of the bag straps. Turn the bag RS out and sew the remaining seams on the outside using blanket stitch.

New skills/blanket stitch

This is a great stitch for embellishing knitted edges and creating decorative seams. It also reinforces them and helps to stop them from curling.

1 Working about ¼" (5 mm) from the edge, take the needle from front to back through the fabric. Move the needle 1 stitch along the edge, then thread from front to back again.

2 Point the needle up, catching the yarn around it, and pull through. Continue along the whole seam.

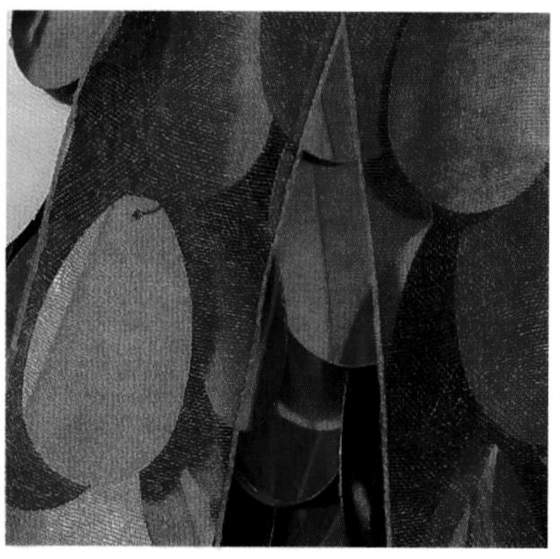

Project 8: Sequined flapper bag

This stunning little evening bag was inspired by the flapper girl dresses of the 1920s, and the sequins really bring it to life. The bag's shape and structure are achieved by slight shaping at the base and knitting with a combination of mercerized cotton yarn and wire to give the bag a sculptural quality. Sheer ribbon is used for the drawstring and handle to complete the high-glam look.

PANELS (make 2)

Thread 141 sequins onto the copper wire. Using size 3 (3.25 mm) needles and yarn, cast on 35 sts. Work the following instructions using both the yarn and wire together.

Row 1 (RS): Knit.

Row 2 & all unspecified WS rows: K1, purl to last st, k1.

Row 3: K1, (seq 1, k3) to last 2 sts, seq 1, k1.

Row 5: (K3, seq 1) to last 3 sts, k3.

Row 7: K1, m1, (seq 1, k3) to last 2 sts, seq 1, m1, k1 (37 sts).

Row 9: K4, (seq 1, k3) to last 5 sts, seq 1, k4.

Row 11: K1, m1, k1, (seq 1, k3) to last 3 sts, seq 1, k1, m1, k1 (39 sts).

Row 13: K1, (seq 1, k3) to last 2 sts, seq 1, k1.

Row 15: (K3, seq 1) to last 3 sts, k3.

Rows 17–24: Repeat rows 13–16 twice.

Rows 25–26: Repeat rows 13–14 once.

Row 27: K7, (seq 1, k7) to end.

Row 29: Knit.

Row 31: K3, (seq 1, k7) to last 4 sts, seq 1, k3.

Row 33: Knit.

Row 35: K7, (seq 1, k7) to end.

Row 37: Knit.

Rows 39–54: Repeat rows 31–38 twice.

Row 55: K1, k2tog, yo, *k3, k2tog, yo, repeat from * to last st, k1.

Rows 57–61: Beginning with a knit row, work five rows in stockinette stitch, keeping the edge stitches as set in previous WS rows.

Row 62: K2tog, purl to last st, k1 (38 sts). Break off wire.

Work the picot bind-off as follows: Bind off 2 sts, *slip remaining st from right needle to left needle, cast on 2 sts, bind off 4 sts; repeat from * until there is 1 st on each needle. Bind off in the usual way and fasten off.

FINISHING

Weave in all any loose ends, then block and steam gently. With RS together, backstitch the pieces together around the

before you start

MEASUREMENTS

6" (15 cm) wide x 6¼" (16 cm) long excluding handle

YARN

Light-weight yarn (100% cotton; approx. 137 yds/115 m per 2 oz/50 g ball) x 1 ball (red)

126 yds (115 m) of 0.2 mm red enameled copper wire

SEQUINS AND NOTIONS

290 x 1" (26 mm) long red oval sequins

1 yd (1 m) of 2½" (6 cm) wide sheer red ribbon for handle

4' (1.2 m) of 1" (2.5 cm) wide sheer red ribbon for drawstring

NEEDLES

Size 3 (3.25 mm)

GAUGE

26 sts x 36 rows = 4" (10 cm) in stockinette stitch using size 3 (3.25 mm) needles

ABBREVIATIONS

k—knit; m1—make 1 stitch by picking up horizontal bar before next stitch and knitting into back of it; RS—right side; seq 1—place 1 sequin and slip 1 stitch purlwise; st(s)—stitch(es); tog—together; WS—wrong side; yo—yarn over

NOTE: Working with wire

This project is knitted with the cotton yarn and copper wire together to give the fabric a rigid quality, but this can take some getting used to. It is therefore even more important than usual to knit a gauge swatch, not only to achieve the correct gauge but also to get a feel for the materials. The holes in the sequins are small, so they are threaded onto the wire only.

sides and base, taking care not to trap sequins in the seam. Turn the bag RS out. Cut the piece of ribbon for the handle in half, place one on top of the other, and use a sewing machine and matching sewing thread to sew both pieces of ribbon together along all edges. Position the strengthened handle so that each end extends 2" (5 cm) inside the top edge of the bag, with the side seams of the bag in the center of the ribbon. Sew in place with sewing thread. Thread the narrower length of ribbon through the lace holes around the top of the bag, starting and ending at the center front. Tie the ribbon in a bow to fasten the bag.

This little bag is the perfect place to use large, show-stopping sequins. These will shimmer and catch the light as you move, and make a delightful noise as well.

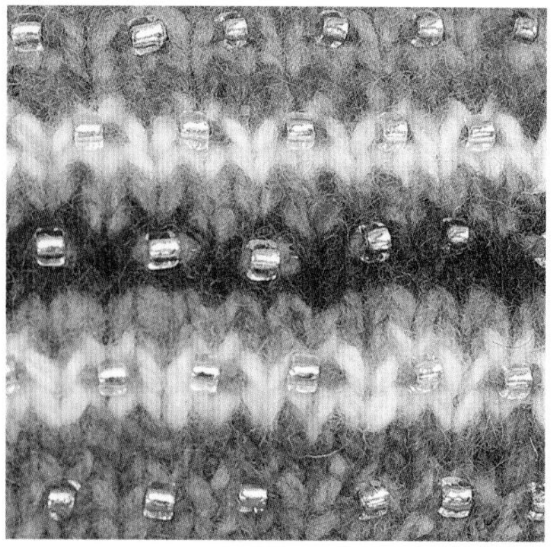

Project 9: Felted bag and change purse

Although made from simple rectangles with no shaping, this bag and change purse use basic techniques to create different but complementary looks. The bag is worked mainly in one color, with squares of beading placed in an irregular design. The contrast yarns used in the handles are threaded through the lace holes in the bag before felting to add layers of sculptural texture. The purse is simply a clever way of making good use of the leftover yarn.

before you start

MEASUREMENTS

Bag 11½" (29 cm) wide x 13" (33 cm) long excluding handle

Purse 5¾" (14.5 cm) wide x 4" (10 cm) long

YARN

DK-weight tweed-effect yarn (100% pure new wool; approx. 123 yds/113 m per 2 oz/50 g ball) in 5 colors:

A Aqua x 3 balls
B Pink x 1 ball
C White x 1 ball
D Green x 1 ball
E Brown x 1 ball

BEADS AND NOTIONS

636 x 3 mm clear beads
6" (15 cm) light-weight closed-end zipper

NEEDLES

Size 9 (5.5 mm); size 8 (5 mm)

GAUGE

17 sts x 23 rows = 4" (10 cm) in stockinette stitch using size 9 (5.5 mm) needles before felting; 18 sts x 30 rows = 4" (10 cm) after felting

ABBREVIATIONS

bead 1—place 1 bead and slip 1 stitch purlwise; k—knit; p—purl; RS—right side; st(s)—stitch(es); tog—together; WS—wrong side; yo—yarn over

BAG PANELS (make 2)

Thread 230 beads onto yarn A. Using size 9 (5.5 mm) needles and yarn A, cast on 61 sts. Beginning at the bottom right of the chart on page 71, work the panel, placing beads and lace holes as indicated. When row 100 of the chart has been completed, work the top ribbing using size 8 (5 mm) needles. Bind off in rib using yarn E.

BAG HANDLES (make 2)

Using size 9 (5.5 mm) needles and yarn E, cast on 79 sts.
Row 1 (RS): Knit.
Row 2: Purl.
Break off yarn E and join yarn B.
Rows 3–4: Repeat rows 1–2.
Break off yarn B and join yarn C.
Rows 5–6: Repeat rows 1–2.
Break off yarn C and join yarn D.
Rows 7–8: Repeat rows 1–2.
Without breaking off yarn D, join yarn A.
Rows 9–10: Repeat rows 1–2 using yarn A.
Break off yarn A and continue using yarn D.
Rows 11–12: Repeat rows 1–2.
Break off yarn D and join yarn C.
Rows 13–14: Repeat rows 1–2.
Break off yarn C and join yarn B.
Rows 15–16: Repeat rows 1–2.
Break off yarn B and join yarn E.
Rows 17–18: Repeat rows 1–2.
Bind off using yarn E.

PURSE PANELS (make 2)

Thread 38 beads onto yarn B and 50 beads onto yarn D. Using size 9 (5.5 mm) needles and yarn D, cast on 29 sts and purl one row. Beginning at the bottom right of the chart on page 70, work the panel, placing beads and changing colors as indicated. When the last row of the chart has been completed, bind off purlwise using yarn E.

This bag and purse are perfect for using up leftover scraps of yarn from other projects, so all you need to buy is the main background color for the bag. Just be sure that the yarns you use are of the same weight and are suitable for felting.

FINISHING—before felting

Weave in any loose ends. Place the bag pieces RS together and backstitch one side seam, taking care to match the stripes at the top. Using the photograph of the bag on page 69 as a guide, thread four ends of yarn B through the vertical lace holes, starting just below the top rib and ending at the cast-on edge of the panel. Secure with a knot on the inside at both ends, taking care not to pull too tightly. Repeat for the remaining vertical lace holes, using the other contrast colors. Run the contrast colors through the horizontal lace holes in the same way, working across both front and back panels. With RS together, sew the remaining side and bottom seams. Fold the handles lengthwise with WS together and overcast the edges together using yarn E. To keep small pieces like the handles and purse together in the wash, thread a piece of scrap cotton yarn through the edges of all pieces and tie together loosely.

FINISHING—after felting

Felt all of the pieces. Remove the cotton yarn and allow the bag and purse pieces to dry thoroughly, then block and steam gently. Position the handles 2¾" (7 cm) in from the side seams and 2" (5 cm) below the top edges of the bag and sew in place on the WS. Position the zipper in the bind-off edges of the purse panels and sew in place. Open the zipper, then with RS together, backstitch the purse's side and bottom seams. Turn the purse RS out.

Purse

KEY (both charts)

- k on RS, p on WS
- p on RS, k on WS
- bead 1
- k2tog
- yo
- A—aqua
- B—pink
- C—white
- D—green
- E—brown

27
25
23
21
19
17
15
13
11
9
7
5
3
1 (RS)

New skills

Felting, see page 45

New skills/inserting a zipper

Inserting a zipper can seem like a tricky process, but if you take your time and do not stretch the fabric, it is actually simple to do.

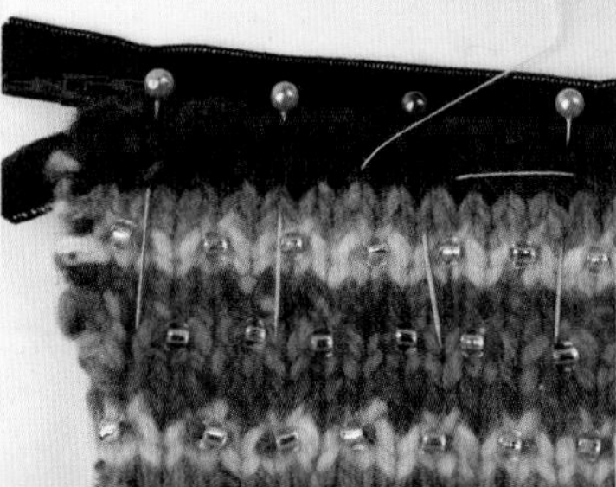

1 With the right side of the knitted fabric facing you, carefully pin the zipper into position so that the edges of the knitted fabric cover the zipper teeth. Baste it in place with a running stitch using a sharp sewing needle and thread. Remove the pins.

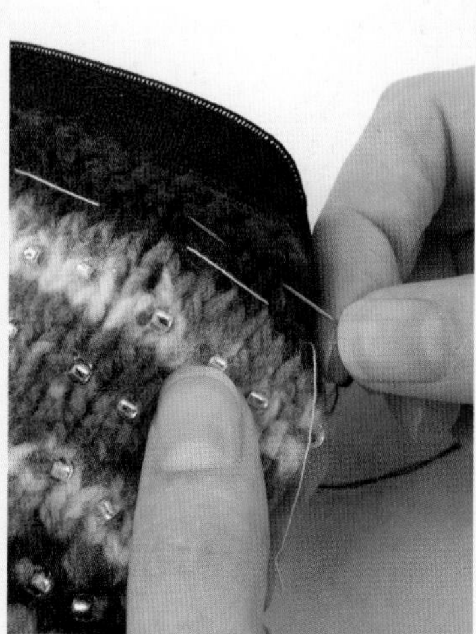

2 Sew the zipper in place using backstitch. If the yarn is too thick and bulky to sew the zipper, try a thinner yarn in the same color, or use matching colored sewing thread. Use the knitting stitches and rows as a guideline to help keep the zipper straight and even.

Bag

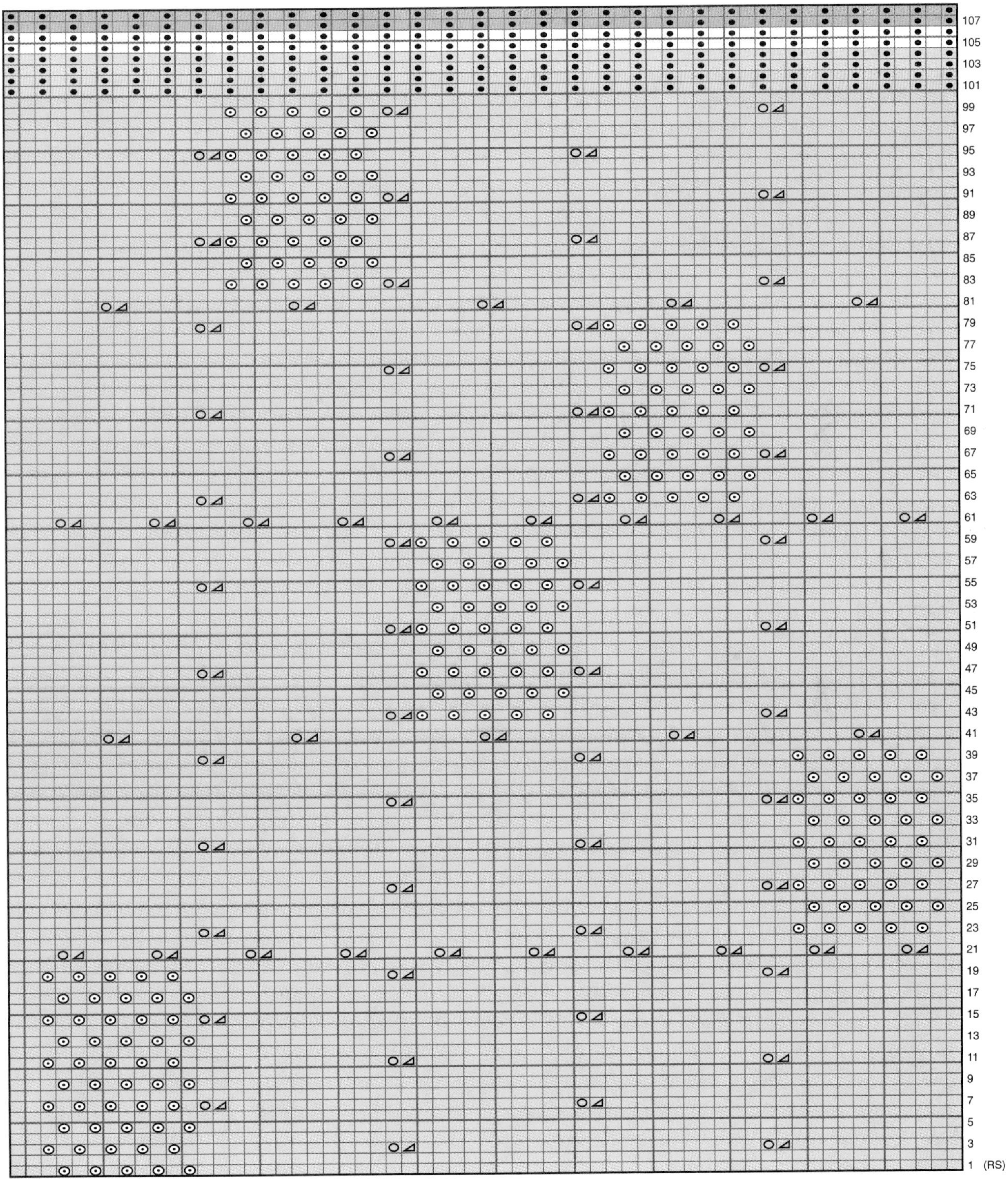

107
105
103
101
99
97
95
93
91
89
87
85
83
81
79
77
75
73
71
69
67
65
63
61
59
57
55
53
51
49
47
45
43
41
39
37
35
33
31
29
27
25
23
21
19
17
15
13
11
9
7
5
3
1 (RS)

Project 10: Dotty denim bag

This bag is great for casual wear but also classic enough for more formal occasions. Choose a decorative lining with a floral design to complement the corsage embellishment. Knitted in denim yarn, which is designed to fade with each wash, the texture and beading become more apparent as the bag ages.

PANELS (make 2)

Thread the beads onto the yarn in the correct sequence (see page 74). Using size 3 (3.25 mm) needles, cast on 67 sts. Work from the chart on page 75, starting at the bottom right, and placing beads and shaping the sides as indicated.

On increase rows: K1, m1, work according to chart to last st, m1, k1.

On decrease rows: K2tog tbl, work according to chart to last st, k2tog.

When the final row of the chart has been completed, bind off purlwise.

HANDLES (make 2)

Thread 79 clear beads onto the yarn. Using size 3 (3.25 mm) needles, cast on 161 sts.

Row 1 (RS): Knit.

Rows 2–8: Beginning with a purl row, work seven rows in stockinette stitch.

Row 9: *K1, bead 1, repeat from * to last st, k1.

Rows 10–16: Beginning with a purl row, work seven rows in stockinette stitch.

Bind off purlwise.

CORSAGE PETALS (make 5)

Thread 4 beads onto the yarn. Using size 3 (3.25 mm) needles, cast on 11 sts.

Row 1 (RS): Knit.

Row 2: Purl.

Row 3: K1, m1, knit to last 2 sts, k2tog.

Row 4: Purl.

Rows 5–6: Repeat rows 3–4 once.

Row 7: K1, m1, (bead 1, k1) 4 times, k1, k2tog.

Row 8: Purl.

Row 9: K2tog, knit to last st, m1, k1.

Row 10: Purl.

Rows 11–14: Repeat rows 9–10 twice.

Bind off purlwise.

CORSAGE BASE

Using size 3 (3.25 mm) needles, cast on 5 sts.

Row 1 (RS): Knit.

Row 2 & all unspecified WS rows: Purl.

Row 3: K1, m1, k3, m1, k1 (7 sts).

Row 5: K1, m1, k5, m1, k1 (9 sts).

Row 7: K1, m1, k7, m1, k1 (11 sts).

Rows 9–12: Repeat rows 1–2 twice.

Row 13: K2tog, knit to last st, k2tog (9 sts).

Rows 15–18: Repeat rows 13–14 twice.

Bind off remaining 5 sts knitwise.

before you start

MEASUREMENTS

11" (28 cm) wide x 7" (18 cm) long excluding handles x 1⅛" (3 cm) deep

YARN

DK-weight yarn (100% cotton denim; approx. 102 yds/93 m per 2 oz/50 g ball) x 4 balls (blue)

BEADS AND NOTIONS

78 x 3 mm white beads, 248 x 3 mm clear beads, and 70 x 3 mm green beads for bag

1 x 8 mm red bead, 20 x 3 mm green beads, and 50 x 3 mm white beads for corsage

30 x 20" (75 x 50 cm) lining fabric

1¼" (3 cm) long pin clip

NEEDLES

Size 3 (3.25 mm)

GAUGE

23 sts x 35 rows = 4" (10 cm) in stockinette stitch using size 3 (3.25 mm) needles before washing; 23 sts x 40 rows = 4" (10 cm) after washing

ABBREVIATIONS

bead 1—place 1 bead and slip 1 stitch purlwise; k—knit; m1—make 1 stitch by picking up horizontal bar before next stitch and knitting into back of it; p—purl; RS—right side; st(s)—stitches; tbl—through back of loop; tog—together; WS—wrong side

NOTE: Using denim yarn

This yarn is designed to shrink in length and fade in appearance like a favorite pair of jeans. This shrinkage has been allowed for in the pattern. It is worth taking time to knit a gauge swatch and wash it according to the instructions on the ball band of the yarn in order to match the post-wash gauge stated in the pattern.

The flower corsage is the perfect finishing touch for this bag. Attached to the bag with a pin clip, you could choose to pin the corsage to your outfit if you prefer. For alternative corsage ideas, see pages 116–117.

New skills

Tassel fringe, see page 96

TIP: Beading sequence
When knitting with beads of more than one color, remember to thread them onto the yarn before casting on in the reverse order to the order in which you will be knitting them. To figure out the correct sequence in which you should thread the beads onto the yarn, follow the chart from the top and read down from left to right on each of the beading rows.

The beading sequence for this bag is: 1 green, (1 white, 1 clear, 1 green) 10 times, 1 white, 1 clear, (1 white, 1 clear, 1 green) twice, 1 white, (1 green, 1 white, 1 clear) twice, (1 white, 1 clear, 1 green) twice, 1 white, (1 green, 1 white, 1 clear) twice, *(1 white, 1 clear, 1 green) twice, 1 white, (1 clear, 1 green, 1 white) twice, 1 clear, 1 green, repeat from * once, (1 white, 1 clear, 1 green) twice, 1 white, (1 green, 1 white, 1 clear) twice, (1 white, 1 clear, 1 green) twice, 1 white

PREPARING THE PIECES

Weave in any loose ends and wash all the pieces with enough spare yarn for sewing up the bag, handles, and corsage. To prevent small pieces like the corsage petals and base from getting lost in the wash, thread a piece of scrap cotton yarn through the edges of all the pieces and tie together loosely. After washing, remove the scrap yarn, allow the pieces to dry thoroughly, then block and steam gently.

FINISHING THE BAG

Using the knitted panels as templates, cut two pieces of lining fabric the same size and shape, adding a 1" (2.5 cm) seam allowance all around. With RS of knitted panels together, backstitch the base seam. Match the top edges and bottom corners and backstitch the side seams. Flatten the bag from the side seams toward the base seam and sew the remaining seams at the bottom corners. Fold the handles WS together and overcast the edges. Position the handles 2" (5 cm) in from side seams and 2" (5 cm) below the top edge on the inside of the bag. Sew in place with the beaded edge of the handles facing outward. With RS of the lining pieces together, sew the base seam using a sewing machine or needle and thread. Match up the top edges and sew the side seams from top edge to bottom corners. Flatten the lining from the side seams toward the base seam and sew the remaining seams at the bottom corners. Fold down the top edges and press the hem to the WS. Trim the seam allowances for a less bulky finish, then place the lining inside the finished bag. Overcast the pressed hem of the lining to the top edge of the bag.

FINISHING THE CORSAGE

Pull together the two points at the left side of each petal and use some of the washed denim yarn to sew the inner dart seam to form a petal shape. Cut a piece of lining fabric the same shape as the corsage base, adding a ⅜" (1 cm) seam allowance. Sew the fabric and knitted base together using matching colored thread and folding the seam allowance under as you sew. Arrange the petals evenly onto the knitted base and sew in place using denim yarn. Cut eight 3–5" (8–12 cm) lengths of washed denim yarn, knot one end of each strand, and thread with beads in a random design. Fold the strands in half so that the beads are at one end, then apply to the center of the corsage using the same technique as applying a tassel fringe. Sew a pin clip to the fabric base using matching sewing thread.

KEY

- ☐ k on RS, p on WS
- [•] p on RS, k on WS
- [◎] bead 1—white
- [◉] bead 1—clear
- [·] bead 1—green

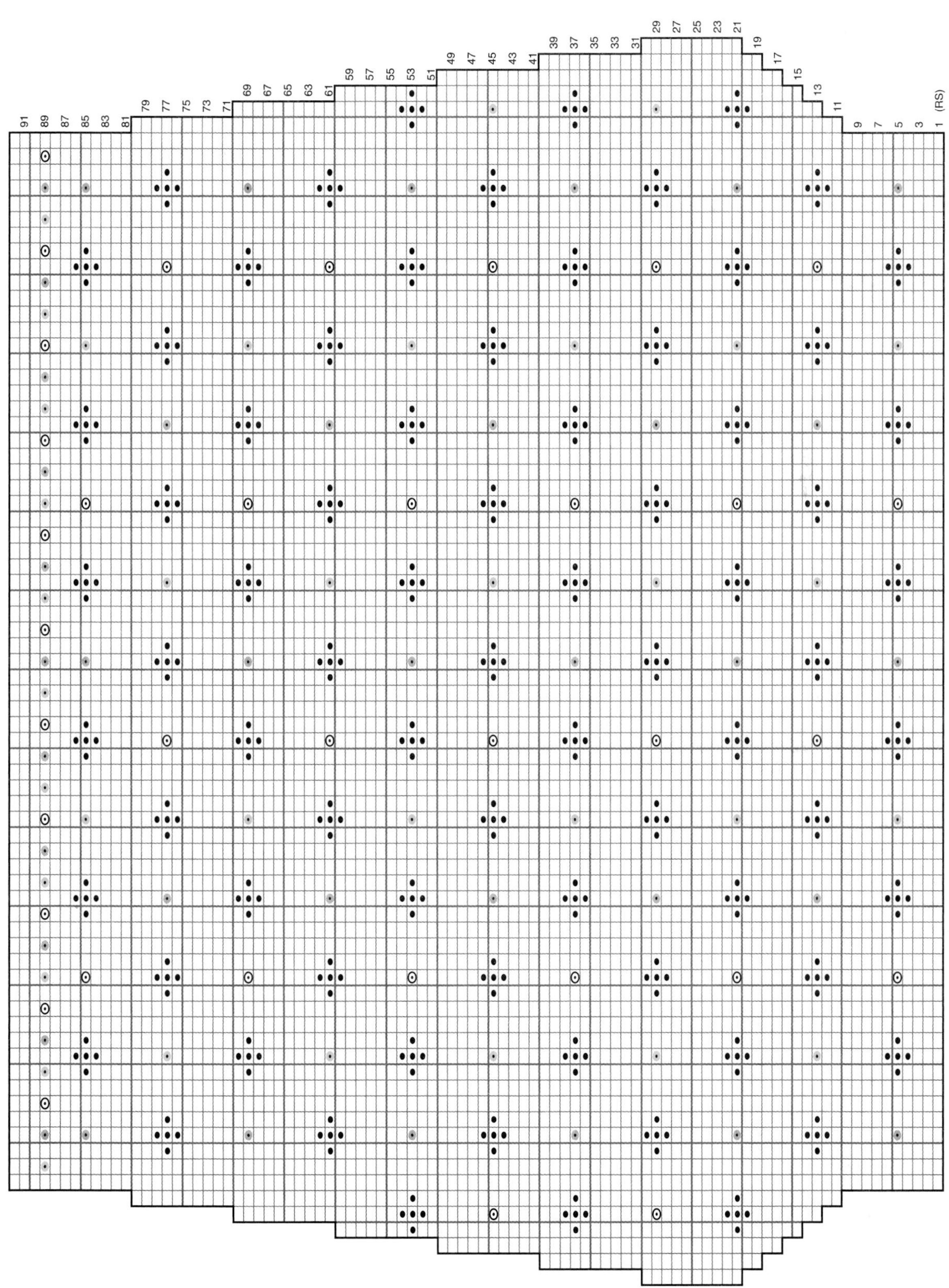
1 (RS)
3
5
7
9
11
13
15
17
19
21
23
25
27
29
31
33
35
37
39
41
43
45
47
49
51
53
55
57
59
61
63
65
67
69
71
73
75
77
79
81
83
85
87
89
91

Project 11: Beaded float skirt

Beads help to give this classic denim skirt a more dressy look. Knitted in indigo-dyed denim yarn, it is worked in a simple pattern that combines beaded floats with dashes of purl stitch texture. Scraps of denim fabric have been used to make the pockets. Instructions for each of the four sizes are given separately in order to make them easier for beginners to follow.

EXTRA SMALL SKIRT PANELS (make 2)

Thread the first batch of beads onto the yarn. Using size 6 (4 mm) needles, cast on 102 sts. Start by working the six rows that form the hem.

Row 1 (RS): K1, bead 6, k6, *bead 4, k6, bead 8, k6, repeat from * to last 17 sts, bead 4, k6, bead 6, k1.

Row 2: Purl.

Row 3: K1, *bead 4, k6, bead 8, k6, repeat from * to last 5 sts, bead 4, k1.

Row 4: Knit.

Row 5: Knit each stitch, wrapping yarn around needle 3 times for each stitch.

Row 6: Knit each stitch, dropping extra loops from yarn wraps of previous row.

Main section

Row 7 (RS): K1, bead 6, k6, *p4, k6, bead 8, k6, repeat from * to last 17 sts, p4, k6, bead 6, k1.

Row 8 & all unspecified WS rows: Purl.

Row 9: K1, *bead 4, k6, p8, k6, repeat from * to last 5 sts, bead 4, k1.

Rows 11–18: Beginning with a knit row, work eight rows in stockinette stitch.

Row 19: K1, *p4, k6, bead 8, k6, repeat from * to last 5 sts, p4, k1.

Row 21: P7, k6, *bead 4, k6, p8, k6, repeat from * to last 17 sts, bead 4, k6, p7.

Rows 23–30: Beginning with a knit row, work eight rows in stockinette stitch.

Row 31: As row 7.

Row 33: As row 9.

Row 35: Knit.

Row 37: K1, k2tog tbl, knit to last 3 sts, k2tog, k1 (100 sts).

Rows 39–42: Beginning with a knit row, work four rows in stockinette stitch.

Row 43: *P4, k6, bead 8, k6, repeat from * to last 4 sts, p4.

Row 45: P6, k6, *bead 4, k6, p8, k6, repeat from * to last 16 sts, bead 4, k6, p6.

NOTE: Using denim yarn

This yarn is designed to shrink in length and fade in appearance like a favorite pair of jeans. This shrinkage has been allowed for in the pattern. It is worth taking time to knit a gauge swatch and wash it according to the instructions on the ball band of the yarn in order to match the post-wash gauge stated in the pattern.

before you start

MEASUREMENTS

Extra small [small, medium, large]
Extra small = To fit hips 34–36" (86–91 cm); actual hip size 35½" (90 cm)
Small = To fit hips 36–38" (91–97 cm); actual hip size 39" (99 cm)
Medium = To fit hips 38–40" (97–102 cm); actual hip size 42½" (108 cm)
Large = To fit hips 40–42" (102–107 cm); actual hip size 45" (114 cm)
All sizes = 23¼" (59 cm) long

YARN

DK-weight yarn (100% cotton denim; approx. 102 yds/93 m per 2 oz/50 g ball) x 9 [10, 12, 14] balls (indigo)

BEADS AND NOTIONS

626 [681, 700, 777] x 3 mm green beads for skirt panels
96 extra beads for waist tie
Two 5½" (14 cm) squares of denim fabric or pockets from an old pair of jeans

NEEDLES

Size 6 (4 mm)

GAUGE

20 sts x 28 rows = 4" (10 cm) in stockinette stitch using size 6 (4 mm) needles before washing; 20 sts x 33 rows = 4" (10 cm) after washing

ABBREVIATIONS

bead—place specified number of beads and slip same number of stitches purlwise; k—knit; p—purl; RS—right side; st(s)—stitch(es); tbl—through back of loop; tog—together; WS—wrong side

TIP: Beading in batches

This pattern uses a lot of beads with areas of plain knitting in between, so you may find it easier to thread the beads onto the yarn in batches of about 100 at a time, breaking off and rejoining the yarn as necessary to thread on more beads.

Rows 47–54: Beginning with a knit row, work eight rows in stockinette stitch.

Row 55: K1, bead 5, k6, *p4, k6, bead 8, k6, repeat from * to last 16 sts, p4, k6, bead 5, k1.

Row 57: K1, bead 3, k6, *p8, k6, bead 4, k6, repeat from * to last 18 sts, p8, k6, bead 3, k1.

Rows 59–66: Beginning with a knit row, work eight rows in stockinette stitch.

Row 67: P1, p2tog, p1, k6, *bead 8, k6, p4, k6, repeat from * to last 18 sts, bead 8, k6, p1, p2tog, p1 (98 sts).

Row 69: P5, k6, bead 4, *k6, p8, k6, bead 4, repeat from * to last 11 sts, k6, p5.

Rows 71–78: Beginning with a knit row, work eight rows in stockinette stitch.

Row 79: K1, bead 4, k6, p4, *k6, bead 8, k6, p4, repeat from * to last 11 sts, k6, bead 4, k1.

Row 81: K1, bead 2, k6, p8, *k6, bead 4, k6, p8, repeat from * to last 9 sts, k6, bead 2, k1.

Rows 83–96: Beginning with a knit row, work fourteen rows in stockinette stitch.

Row 97: K1, k2tog tbl, knit to last 3 sts, k2tog, k1 (96 sts).

Row 99: P2, k6, bead 8, *k6, p4, k6, bead 8, repeat from * to last 8 sts, k6, p2.

Row 101: P4, k6, bead 4, *k6, p8, k6, bead 4, repeat from * to last 10 sts, k6, p4.

The beads float across the skirt to add movement to the design, and look especially good where they dangle below the hemline.

Rows 103–118: Beginning with a knit row, work sixteen rows in stockinette stitch.
Row 119: K1, bead 3, k6, p4, *k6, bead 8, k6, p4, repeat from * to last 10 sts, k6, bead 3, k1.
Row 121: K1, bead 1, k6, p8, *k6, bead 4, k6, p8, repeat from * to last 8 sts, k6, bead 1, k1.
Rows 123–126: Beginning with a knit row, work four rows in stockinette stitch.
Row 127: K1, k2tog tbl, knit to last 3 sts, k2tog, k1 (94 sts).
Rows 129–138: Beginning with a knit row, work ten rows in stockinette stitch.
Row 139: P1, k6, bead 8, k6, *p4, k6, bead 8, k6, repeat from * to last st, k1.

Shaping darts

Row 141 (RS): P3, k6, bead 4, k9, k2tog tbl, k2tog, k7, bead 4, k6, p8, k6, bead 4, k7, k2tog tbl, k2tog, k9, bead 4, k6, p3 (90 sts).
Rows 143–158: Beginning with a knit row, work sixteen rows in stockinette stitch.
Row 159: K1, bead 2, k6, p4, k18, p4, k6, bead 8, k6, p4, k18, p4, k6, bead 2, k1.
Row 161: K7, p8, k14, p8, k6, bead 4, k6, p8, k14, p8, k7.
Rows 163–166: Beginning with a knit row, work four rows in stockinette stitch.
Row 167: K21, k2tog tbl, k2tog, k40, k2tog tbl, k2tog, knit to end (86 sts).
Rows 169–180: Beginning with a knit row, work twelve rows in stockinette stitch.
Row 181: Knit.
Row 182: Knit.
Row 183: Knit each stitch, wrapping yarn around needle 3 times for each stitch.
Row 184: Knit each stitch, dropping extra loops from yarn wraps of previous row.
Rows 185–188: Beginning with a knit row, work four rows in stockinette stitch.
Bind off knitwise.

SMALL SKIRT PANELS (make 2)

Thread the first batch of beads onto the yarn. Using size 6 (4 mm) needles, cast on 111 sts. Start by working the six rows that form the hem.
Row 1 (RS): K4, *bead 8, k6, bead 4, k6, repeat from * to last 11 sts, bead 8, k3.
Row 2: Purl.
Row 3: K6, *bead 4, k6, bead 8, k6, repeat from * to last 9 sts, bead 4, k5.
Row 4: Knit.
Row 5: Knit each stitch, wrapping yarn around needle 3 times for each stitch.
Row 6: Knit each stitch, dropping extra loops from yarn wraps of previous row.

Main section

Row 7 (RS): K4, bead 8, *k6, p4, k6, bead 8, repeat from * to last 3 sts, k3.
Row 8 & all unspecified WS rows: Purl.
Row 9: K6, *bead 4, k6, p8, k6, repeat from * to last 9 sts, bead 4, k5.
Rows 11–18: Beginning with a knit row, work eight rows in stockinette stitch.
Row 19: K6, *p4, k6, bead 8, k6, repeat from * to last 9 sts, p4, k5.
Row 21: K4, *p8, k6, bead 4, k6, repeat from * to last 11 sts, p8, k3.
Rows 23–30: Beginning with a knit row, work eight rows in stockinette stitch.
Row 31: As row 7.
Row 33: As row 9.
Row 35: Knit.
Row 37: K1, k2tog tbl, knit to last 3 sts, k2tog, k1 (109 sts).
Rows 39–42: Beginning with a knit row, work four rows in stockinette stitch.
Row 43: K5, *p4, k6, bead 8, k6, repeat from * to last 8 sts, p4, k4.
Row 45: K3, *p8, k6, bead 4, k6, repeat from * to last 10 sts, p8, k2.
Rows 47–54: Beginning with a knit row, work eight rows in stockinette stitch.
Row 55: K3, *bead 8, k6, p4, k6, repeat from * to last 10 sts, bead 8, k2.
Row 57: K5, *bead 4, k6, p8, k6, repeat from * to last 8 sts, bead 4, k4.
Rows 59–66: Beginning with a knit row, work eight rows in stockinette stitch.
Row 67: K1, k2tog, k2, *p4, k6, bead 8, k6, repeat from * to last 8 sts, p4, k1, k2tog, k1 (107 sts).
Row 69: K2, *p8, k6, bead 4, k6, repeat from * to last 9 sts, p8, k1.
Rows 71–78: Beginning with a knit row, work eight rows in stockinette stitch.
Row 79: K2, *bead 8, k6, p4, k6, repeat from * to last 9 sts, bead 8, k1.
Row 81: K4, *bead 4, k6, p8, k6, repeat from * to last 7 sts, bead 4, k3.
Rows 83–96: Beginning with a knit row, work fourteen rows in stockinette stitch.
Row 97: K1, k2tog tbl, knit to last 3 sts, k2tog, k1 (105 sts).
Row 99: K3, *p4, k6, bead 8, k6, repeat from * to last 6 sts, p4, k2.
Row 101: K1, *p8, k6, bead 4, k6, repeat from * to last 8 sts, p8.
Rows 103–118: Beginning with a knit row, work sixteen rows in stockinette stitch.
Row 119: K1, *bead 8, k6, p4, k6, repeat from * to last 8 sts, bead 7, k1.
Row 121: K3, *bead 4, k6, p8, k6, repeat from * to last 6 sts, bead 4, k2.
Rows 123–126: Beginning with a knit row, work four rows in stockinette stitch.
Row 127: K1, k2tog tbl, knit to last 3 sts, k2tog, k1 (103 sts).
Rows 129–138: Beginning with a knit row, work ten rows in stockinette stitch.
Row 139: K2, *p4, k6, bead 8, k6, repeat from * to last 5 sts, p4, k1.

Shaping darts

Row 141 (RS): P8, k6, bead 4, k6, k2tog tbl, k2tog, k10, bead 4, k6, p8, k6, bead 4, k10, k2tog tbl, k2tog, k6, bead 4, k6, p7 (99 sts).
Rows 143–158: Beginning with a knit row, work sixteen rows in stockinette stitch.
Row 159: K1, bead 7, k6, p4, k18, p4, k6, bead 8, k6, p4, k18, p4, k6, bead 6, k1.
Row 161: K2, bead 4, k6, p8, k14, p8, k6, bead 4, k6, p8, k14, p8, k6, bead 4, k1.
Rows 163–166: Beginning with a knit row, work four rows in stockinette stitch.
Row 167: K23, k2tog tbl, k2tog, k46, k2tog tbl, k2tog, knit to end (95 sts).
Rows 169–180: Beginning with a knit row, work twelve rows in stockinette stitch.
Row 181: Knit.
Row 182: Knit.
Row 183: Knit each stitch, wrapping yarn around needle 3 times for each stitch.
Row 184: Knit each stitch, dropping extra loops from yarn wraps of previous row.

Rows 185–188: Beginning with a knit row, work four rows in stockinette stitch.
Bind off knitwise.

MEDIUM SKIRT PANELS (make 2)

Thread the first batch of beads onto the yarn. Using size 6 (4 mm) needles, cast on 119 sts. Start by working the six rows that form the hem.

Row 1 (RS): K1, bead 1, k6, *bead 8, k6, bead 4, k6, repeat from * to last 15 sts, bead 8, k7.
Row 2: Purl.
Row 3: K1, bead 3, k6, *bead 4, k6, bead 8, k6, repeat from * to last 13 sts, bead 4, k6, bead 2, k1.
Row 4: Knit.
Row 5: Knit each stitch, wrapping yarn around needle 3 times for each stitch.
Row 6: Knit each stitch, dropping extra loops from yarn wraps of previous row.

Main section

Row 7 (RS): P2, k6, bead 8, *k6, p4, k6, bead 8, repeat from * to last 7 sts, k6, p1.
Row 8 & all WS unspecified rows: Purl.
Row 9: P4, k6, bead 4, *k6, p8, k6, bead 4, repeat from * to last 9 sts, k6, p3.
Rows 11–18: Beginning with a knit row, work eight rows in stockinette stitch.
Row 19: K1, bead 3, k6, p4, *k6, bead 8, k6, p4, repeat from * to last 9 sts, k6, bead 2, k1.
Row 21: K1, bead 1, k6, p8, *k6, bead 4, k6, p8, repeat from * to last 7 sts, knit to end.
Rows 23–30: Beginning with a knit row, work eight rows in stockinette stitch.
Row 31: As row 7.
Row 33: As row 9.
Row 35: Knit.
Row 37: K1, k2tog tbl, knit to last 3 sts, k2tog, k1 (117 sts).
Rows 39–42: Beginning with a knit row, work four rows in stockinette stitch.
Row 43: K1, bead 2, k6, p4, *k6, bead 8, k6, p4, repeat from * to last 8 sts, k6, bead 1, k1.
Row 45: K7, p8, *k6, bead 4, k6, p8, repeat from * to last 6 sts, knit to end.
Rows 47–54: Beginning with a knit row, work eight rows in stockinette stitch.
Row 55: P1, k6, bead 8, *k6, p4, k6, bead 8, repeat from * to last 6 sts, knit to end.
Row 57: P3, k6, bead 4, *k6, p8, k6, bead 4, repeat from * to last 8 sts, k6, p2.
Rows 59–66: Beginning with a knit row, work eight rows in stockinette stitch.
Row 67: K1, k2tog, k6, p4, *k6, bead 8, k6, p4, repeat from * to last 8 sts, k5, k2tog, k1 (115 sts).
Row 69: K6, p8, *k6, bead 4, k6, p8, repeat from * to last 5 sts, knit to end.
Rows 71–78: Beginning with a knit row, work eight rows in stockinette stitch.
Row 79: K6, bead 8, *k6, p4, k6, bead 8, repeat from * to last 5 sts, knit to end.
Row 81: P2, k6, bead 4, *k6, p8, k6, bead 4, repeat from * to last 7 sts, k6, p1.
Rows 83–96: Beginning with a knit row, work fourteen rows in stockinette stitch.
Row 97: K1, k2tog tbl, knit to last 3 sts, k2tog, k1 (113 sts).
Row 99: K7, p4, *k6, bead 8, k6, p4, repeat from * to last 6 sts, knit to end.
Row 101: K5, p8, *k6, bead 4, k6, p8, repeat from * to last 4 sts, knit to end.
Rows 103–118: Beginning with a knit row, work sixteen rows in stockinette stitch.
Row 119: K5, bead 8, *k6, p4, k6, bead 8, repeat from * to last 4 sts, knit to end.
Row 121: P1, k6, bead 4, *k6, p8, k6, bead 4, repeat from * to last 6 sts, knit to end.
Rows 123–126: Beginning with a knit row, work four rows in stockinette stitch.
Row 127: K1, k2tog tbl, knit to last 3 sts, k2tog, k1 (111 sts).
Rows 129–138: Beginning with a knit row, work ten rows in stockinette stitch.
Row 139: K6, p4, *k6, bead 8, k6, p4, repeat from * to last 5 sts, knit to end.

Shaping darts

Row 141 (RS): K4, p8, k6, bead 4, k4, k2tog tbl, k2tog, k12, bead 4, k6, p8, k6, bead 4, k12, k2tog tbl, k2tog, k4, bead 4, k6, p8, k3 (107 sts).
Rows 143–158: Beginning with a knit row, work sixteen rows in stockinette stitch.
Row 159: K4, bead 8, k6, p4, k18, p4, k6, bead 8, k6, p4, k18, p4, k6, bead 8, k3.
Row 161: K6, bead 4, k6, p8, k14, p8, k6, bead 4, k6, p8, k14, p8, k6, bead 4, k5.
Rows 163–166: Beginning with a knit row, work four rows in stockinette stitch.
Row 167: K25, k2tog tbl, k2tog, k50, k2tog tbl, k2tog, knit to end (103 sts).
Rows 169–180: Beginning with a knit row, work twelve rows in stockinette stitch.
Row 181: Knit.
Row 182: Knit.
Row 183: Knit each stitch, wrapping yarn around needle 3 times for each stitch.
Row 184: Knit each stitch, dropping extra loops from yarn wraps of previous row.
Rows 185–188: Beginning with a knit row, work four rows in stockinette stitch.
Bind off knitwise.

LARGE SKIRT PANELS (make 2)

Thread the first batch of beads onto the yarn. Using size 6 (4 mm) needles, cast on 127 sts. Start by working the six rows that form the hem.

Row 1 (RS): K2, bead 4, *k6, bead 8, k6, bead 4, repeat from * to last st, k1.
Row 2: Purl.
Row 3: K1, bead 7, k6, bead 4, k6, *bead 8, k6, bead 4, k6, repeat from * to last 7 sts, bead 6, k1.
Row 4: Knit.

Row 5: Knit each stitch, wrapping yarn around needle 3 times for each stitch.
Row 6: Knit each stitch, dropping extra loops from yarn wraps of previous row.

Main section

Row 7 (RS): K2, p4, *k6, bead 8, k6, p4, repeat from * to last st, k1.
Row 8 & all unspecified WS rows: Purl.
Row 9: P8, k6, bead 4, k6, *p8, k6, bead 4, k6, repeat from * to last 7 sts, purl to end.
Rows 11–18: Beginning with a knit row, work eight rows in stockinette stitch.
Row 19: K1, bead 7, k6, p4, k6, *bead 8, k6, p4, k6, repeat from * to last 7 sts, bead 6, k1.
Row 21: K2, bead 4, *k6, p8, k6, bead 4, repeat from * to last st, k1.
Rows 23–30: Beginning with a knit row, work eight rows in stockinette stitch.
Row 31: As row 7.
Row 33: As row 9.
Row 35: Knit.
Row 37: K1, k2tog tbl, knit to last 3 sts, k2tog, k1 (125 sts).
Rows 39–42: Beginning with a knit row, work four rows in stockinette stitch.
Row 43: K1, bead 6, k6, p4, k6, *bead 8, k6, p4, k6, repeat from * to last 6 sts, bead 5, k1.
Row 45: K1, *bead 4, k6, p8, k6, repeat from * to last 4 sts, bead 3, k1.
Rows 47–54: Beginning with a knit row, work eight rows in stockinette stitch.
Row 55: K1, *p4, k6, bead 8, k6, repeat from * to last 4 sts, p4.
Row 57: P7, k6, bead 4, k6, *p8, k6, bead 4, k6, repeat from * to last 6 sts, knit to end.
Rows 59–66: Beginning with a knit row, work eight rows in stockinette stitch.

New skills

Twisted cord, see page 51

Row 67: K1, k2tog, bead 4, k6, p4, *k6, bead 8, k6, p4, repeat from * to last 12 sts, k6, bead 3, k2tog, k1 (123 sts).
Row 69: K1, bead 3, k6, p8, k6, *bead 4, k6, p8, k6, repeat from * to last 3 sts, bead 2, k1.
Rows 71–78: Beginning with a knit row, work eight rows in stockinette stitch.
Row 79: P4, k6, bead 8, k6, repeat from * to last 3 sts, p3.
Row 81: P6, k6, bead 4, k6, *p8, k6, bead 4, k6, repeat from * to last 5 sts, k5.
Rows 83–96: Beginning with a knit row, work fourteen rows in stockinette stitch.
Row 97: K1, k2tog tbl, knit to last 3 sts, k2tog, k1 (121 sts).
Row 99: K1, bead 4, k6, p4, k6, *bead 8, k6, p4, k6, repeat from * to last 4 sts, bead 3, k1.
Row 101: K1, bead 2, k6, p8, k6, *bead 4, k6, p8, k6, repeat from * to last 2 sts, bead 1, k1.
Rows 103–118: Beginning with a knit row, work sixteen rows in stockinette stitch.
Row 119: P3, k6, bead 8, k6, *p4, k6, bead 8, k6, repeat from * to last 2 sts, p2.
Row 121: P5, k6, bead 4, k6, *p8, k6, bead 4, k6, repeat from * to last 4 sts, p4.
Rows 123–126: Beginning with a knit row, work four rows in stockinette stitch.
Row 127: K1, k2tog tbl, knit to last 3 sts, k2tog, k1 (119 sts).
Rows 129–138: Beginning with a knit row, work ten rows in stockinette stitch.
Row 139: K1, bead 3, k6, p4, k6, *bead 8, k6, p4, k6, repeat from * to last 3 sts, bead 2, k1.

Shaping darts

Row 141 (RS): K1, bead 1, k6, p8, k6, bead 4, k2, k2tog tbl, k2tog, k14, bead 4, k6, p8, k6, bead 4, k14, k2tog tbl, k2tog, k2, bead 4, k6, p8, k7 (115 sts).
Rows 143–158: Beginning with a knit row, work sixteen rows in stockinette stitch.
Row 159: P2, k6, bead 8, k6, p4, k18, p4, k6, bead 8, k6, p4, k18, p4, k6, bead 8, k6, p1.
Row 161: P4, k6, bead 4, k6, p8, k14, p8, k6, bead 4, k6, p8, k14, p8, k6, bead 4, k6, p3.
Rows 163–166: Beginning with a knit row, work four rows in stockinette stitch.
Row 167: K27, k2tog tbl, k2tog, k54, k2tog tbl, k2tog, knit to end (111 sts).
Rows 169–180: Beginning with a knit row, work twelve rows in stockinette stitch.
Row 181: Knit.
Row 182: Knit.
Row 183: Knit each stitch, wrapping yarn around needle 3 times for each stitch.
Row 184: Knit each stitch, dropping extra loops from yarn wraps of previous row.
Rows 185–188: Beginning with a knit row, work four rows in stockinette stitch.
Bind off knitwise.

FINISHING

Weave in any loose ends. Wash the skirt panels and about 50' (15 m) of yarn to sew the seams and make the waist tie. Allow to dry, then block and steam gently. Cut two 5½" (14 cm) squares of denim fabric or detach two pockets from a pair of old jeans. Fold ¾" (2 cm) of the top edge to the WS and sew in place with contrasting colored sewing thread. Fold the three remaining edges to the WS by ¾" (2 cm) and position the pockets on the skirt front, matching the center of the pocket bases to the bottom of the dart shaping and taking care that the top hem is parallel to the waist edge. Make sure that the pockets are symmetrically positioned on the front panel. Stitch in place neatly. With RS together, backstitch the front and back skirt panels together using spare washed yarn. Make two 5' (150 cm) long twisted cords, using two strands of yarn for each cord. Knot the two cords together about 4" (10 cm) from each end. Thread the double cord through the drop-stitch row at the waist, beginning and ending at center front. Cut the folded ends of the cord to separate the strands of yarn, then thread six beads onto each strand and knot to secure them in place.

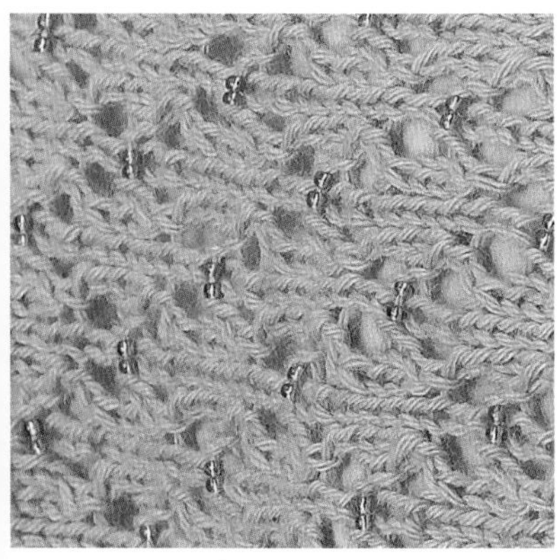

Project 12: Sumptuously soft shrug

This pretty shrug combines a DK-weight alpaca/silk blend yarn with an open-work lace pattern, making it wonderfully soft and feminine. It is knitted in one piece, so there are few seams to sew. The gold beads complement the honey color of the yarn to give the shrug a delicate romantic look.

KNITTING THE SHRUG

Thread 600 [750, 900] beads onto the yarn in batches of 100 at a time, breaking off and rejoining the yarn to thread on more beads as necessary. Using size 8 (5 mm) needles, cast on 55 [61, 67] sts.

Row 1 (RS): K1, *k2tog, yo, k1, yo, k2tog tbl, k1, repeat from * to end.

Row 2 & all unspecified WS rows: Purl.

Row 3: K3 (bead 2, k5) to last 4 sts, bead 2, k3.

Row 5: K1, *k2tog, yo, k1, yo, k2tog tbl, k1, repeat from * to end.

before you start

MEASUREMENTS

Small [medium, large]
To fit bust 32–34 [36, 38–40]" (81–86 [91, 97–102] cm)
Width from cast-on to bind-off edge = 30 [32, 34]" (76 [81, 86] cm)
Length at center back = 16 [16½, 17½]" (40 [42, 44] cm)

YARN

DK-weight yarn (70% alpaca, 30% silk; approx. 289 yds/265 m per 4 oz/100 g ball) x 2 balls (honey)

BEADS

600 [750, 900] x 3 mm gold beads

NEEDLES

Size 8 (5 mm)

GAUGE

17 sts x 20 rows = 4" (10 cm) in beaded lace pattern using size 8 (5 mm) needles

ABBREVIATIONS

bead 2—place 2 beads and slip 1 stitch purlwise; k—knit; m1—make 1 stitch by picking up horizontal bar before next stitch and working into back of it knitwise on a knit row or purlwise on a purl row; p—purl; RS—right side; st(s)—stitch(es); tbl—through back of loop; tog—together; WS—wrong side; yo—yarn over

Row 6: P1, m1, purl to last st, m1, p1 (57 [63, 69] sts).

Row 7: K2, yo, k2tog tbl, k1, *k2tog, yo, k1, yo, k2tog tbl, k1, repeat from * to last 4 sts, k2tog, yo, k2.

Row 8: P1, m1, purl to last st, m1, p1 (59 [65, 71] sts).

Row 9: K2 (bead 2, k5) to last 3 sts, bead 2, k2.

Row 10: P1, m1, purl to last st, m1, p1 (61 [67, 73] sts).

Row 11: K1, *k2tog, yo, k1, yo, k2tog tbl, k1, repeat from * to end.

Row 12: P1, m1, purl to last st, m1, p1 (63 [69, 75] sts).

Row 13: K2, yo, k2tog tbl, k1, *k2tog, yo, k1, yo, k2tog tbl, k1, repeat from * to last 4 sts, k2tog, yo, k2.

Row 14: P1, m1, purl to last st, m1, p1 (65 [71, 77] sts).

Row 15: K2 (bead 2, k5) to last 3 sts, bead 2, k2.

Row 16: P1, m1, purl to last st, m1, p1 (67 [73, 79] sts).
Row 17: K1, *k2tog, yo, k1, yo, k2tog tbl, k1, repeat from * to end.
Row 18: P1, m1, purl to last st, m1, p1 (69 [75, 81] sts).
Row 19: K1, m1, k1, yo, k2tog tbl, k1, *k2tog, yo, k1, yo, k2tog tbl, k1, repeat from * to last 4 sts, k2tog, yo, k1, m1, k1 (71 [77, 83] sts).
Row 20: P1, m1, purl to last st, m1, p1 (73 [79, 85] sts).
Row 21: K1, m1, k2, (bead 2, k5) to last 4 sts, bead 2, k2, m1, k1 (75 [81, 87] sts).
Row 22: P1, m1, purl to last st, m1, p1 (77 [83, 89] sts).
Row 23: K3, *k2tog, yo, k1, yo, k2tog tbl, k1, repeat from * to last 2 sts, k2.
Row 24: P1, m1, purl to last st, m1, p1 (79 [85, 91] sts).
Row 25: K1, *k2tog, yo, k1, yo, k2tog tbl, k1, repeat from * to end.
Row 26: P1, m1, purl to last st, m1, p1 (81 [87, 93] sts). Place markers at beginning and end of row for making up.
Row 27: K4, (bead 2, k5) to last 5 sts, bead 2, k4.
Row 29: K2, *k2tog, yo, k1, yo, k2tog tbl, k1, repeat from * to last st, k1.
Row 31: K2, yo, k2tog tbl, k1, *k2tog, yo, k1, yo, k2tog tbl, k1, repeat from * to last 4 sts, k2tog, yo, k2.
Row 33: K7, (bead 2, k5) to last 8 sts, bead 2, k7.
Row 34: P2tog, purl to last 2 sts, p2tog (79 [85, 91] sts).
Row 35: K1, yo, k2tog tbl, k1, *k2tog, yo, k1, yo, k2tog tbl, k1, repeat from * to last 3 sts, k2tog, yo, k1.
Row 37: K1, *k2tog, yo, k1, yo, k2tog tbl, k1, repeat from * to end.
Row 39: K3 (bead 2, k5) to last 4 sts, bead 2, k3.

The alpaca/silk blend yarn is wonderfully soft and surprisingly warm, so this shrug feels beautiful against the skin while providing a little protection against chills.

Row 40: P2tog, purl to last 2 sts, p2tog (77 [83, 89] sts).
Row 41: *K2tog, yo, k1, yo, k2tog tbl, k1, repeat from * to last 5 sts, k2tog, yo, k1, yo, k2tog tbl.
Row 43: K3, *k2tog, yo, k1, yo, k2tog tbl, k1, repeat from * to last 2 sts, k2.
Row 45: (K5, bead 2) to last 5 sts, k5.
Row 46: P2tog, purl to last 2 sts, p2tog (75 [81, 87] sts).
Row 47: K2, *k2tog, yo, k1, yo, k2tog tbl, k1, repeat from * to last st, k1.
Row 49: K2, yo, k2tog tbl, k1, *k2tog, yo, k1, yo, k2tog tbl, k1, repeat from * to last 4 sts, k2tog, yo, k2.
Row 51: K7, (bead 2, k5) to last 8 sts, bead 2, k7.
Row 52: P2tog, purl to last 2 sts, p2tog (73 [79, 85] sts).
Rows 53–70: Repeat rows 35–52 (67 [73, 79] sts).
Rows 71–75: Repeat rows 35–39.
Row 76: Purl.
Row 77: K1, *k2tog, yo, k1, yo, k2tog tbl, k1, repeat from * to end.
Row 79: K1, yo, k2tog tbl, k1, *k2tog, yo, k1, yo, k2tog tbl, k1, repeat from * to last 3 sts, k2tog, yo, k1.
Row 81: K6, (bead 2, k5) to last st, k1.
Medium size only: Repeat rows 71–82 once.
Large size only: Repeat rows 71–82 twice.
All sizes: Continue pattern as follows.
Row 83: K1, yo, k2tog tbl, k1, *k2tog, yo, k1, yo, k2tog tbl, k1, repeat from * to last 3 sts, k2tog, yo, k1.
Row 85: K1, *k2tog, yo, k1, yo, k2tog tbl, k1, repeat from * to end.
Row 86: P1, m1, purl to last st, m1, p1 (69 [75, 81] sts).
Row 87: K4, (bead 2, k5) to last 5 sts, bead 2, k4.
Row 89: K2, *k2tog, yo, k1, yo, k2tog tbl, k1, repeat from * to last st, k1.
Row 91: K2, *yo, k2tog tbl, k1, k2tog, yo, k1, repeat from * to last st, k1.
Row 92: P1, m1, purl to last st, m1, p1 (71 [77, 83] sts).
Row 93: K2 (bead 2, k5) to last 3 sts, bead 2, k2.
Row 95: *K2tog, yo, k1, yo, k2tog tbl, k1, repeat from * to last 5 sts, k2tog, yo, k1, yo, k2tog tbl.
Row 97: K3, *k2tog, yo, k1, yo, k2tog tbl, k1, repeat from * to last 2 sts, k2.
Row 98: P1, m1, purl to last st, m1, p1 (73 [79, 85] sts).
Row 99: K6, (bead 2, k5) to last st, k1.
Row 101: K1, yo, k2tog tbl, k1, *k2tog, yo, k1, yo, k2tog tbl, k1, repeat from * to last 3 sts, k2tog, yo, k1.
Row 103: K1, *k2tog, yo, k1, yo, k2tog tbl, k1, repeat from * to end.
Row 104: P1, m1, purl to last st, m1, p1 (75 [81, 87] sts).
Row 105: K4, (bead 2, k5) to last 5 sts, bead 2, k4.
Row 107: K2, *k2tog, yo, k1, yo, k2tog tbl, k1, repeat from * to last st, k1.
Row 109: K2, *yo, k2tog tbl, k1, k2tog, yo, k1, repeat from * to last st, k1.
Row 110: P1, m1, purl to last st, m1, p1 (77 [83, 89] sts).
Row 111: K2 (bead 2, k5) to last 3 sts, bead 2, k2.
Row 113: *K2tog, yo, k1, yo, k2tog tbl, k1, repeat from * to last 5 sts, k2tog, yo, k1, yo, k2tog tbl.
Row 115: K3, *k2tog, yo, k1, yo, k2tog tbl, k1, repeat from * to last 2 sts, k2.
Row 116: P1, m1, purl to last st, m1, p1 (79 [85, 91] sts).
Row 117: K6, (bead 2, k5) to last st, k1.
Row 119: K1, yo, k2tog tbl, k1, *k2tog, yo, k1, yo, k2tog tbl, k1, repeat from * to last 3 sts, k2tog, yo, k1.
Row 121: K1, *k2tog, yo, k1, yo, k2tog tbl, k1, repeat from * to end.
Row 122: P1, m1, purl to last st, m1, p1 (81 [87, 93] sts).
Row 123: K4, (bead 2, k5) to last 5 sts, bead 2, k4.
Row 125: K2, *k2tog, yo, k1, yo, k2tog tbl, k1, repeat from * to last st, k1.
Row 127: K2, yo, k2tog tbl, k1, *k2tog, yo, k1, yo, k2tog tbl, k1, repeat from * to last 4 sts, k2tog, yo, k2.
Row 129: K7, (bead 2, k5) to last 8 sts, bead 2, k7.
Row 130: P2tog, purl to last 2 sts, p2tog (79 [85, 91] sts).
Row 131: K1, yo, k2tog tbl, k1, *k2tog, yo, k1, yo, k2tog tbl, k1, repeat from * to last 3 sts, k2tog, yo, k1.
Row 132: P2tog, purl to last 2 sts, p2tog (77 [83, 89] sts).
Row 133: K2tog, k1, yo, k2tog tbl, k1, *k2tog, yo, k1, yo, k2tog tbl, k1, repeat from * to last 5 sts, k2tog, yo, k1, k2tog (75 [81, 87] sts).
Row 134: P2tog, purl to last 2 sts, p2tog (73 [79, 85] sts).
Row 135: K2tog, k4, (bead 2, k5) to last 7 sts, bead 2, k4, k2tog (71 [77, 83] sts).
Row 137: K2tog, k1, *k2tog, yo, k1, yo, k2tog tbl, k1, rep from * to last 2 sts, k2tog (69 [75, 81] sts).
Row 139: K2tog, yo, k2tog tbl, k1, *k2tog, yo, k1, yo, k2tog tbl, k1, repeat from * to last 4 sts, k2tog, yo, k2tog (67 [73, 79] sts).
Row 141: K2tog, k4, (bead 2, k5) to last 7 sts, bead 2, k4, k2tog (65 [71, 77] sts).
Row 143: K2tog, k1, *k2tog, yo, k1, yo, k2tog tbl, k1, repeat from * to last 2 sts, k2tog (63 [69, 75] sts).
Row 145: K2tog, yo, k2tog tbl, k1, *k2tog, yo, k1, yo, k2tog tbl, k1, repeat from * to last 4 sts, k2tog, yo, k2tog (61 [67, 73] sts).
Row 147: K2tog, k4, (bead 2, k5) to last 7 sts, bead 2, k4, k2tog (59 [65, 71] sts).
Row 149: K2tog, k1, *k2tog, yo, k1, yo, k2tog tbl, k1, repeat from * to last 2 sts, k2tog (57 [63, 69] sts).
Row 151: K2tog, yo, k2tog tbl, k1, *k2tog, yo, k1, yo, k2tog tbl, k1, repeat from * to last 4 sts, k2tog, yo, k2tog (55 [61, 67] sts).
Row 153: K6, (bead 2, k5) to last st, k1.
Row 155: K1, yo, k2tog tbl, k1, *k2tog, yo, k1, yo, k2tog tbl, k1, repeat from * to last 3 sts, k2tog, yo, k1.
Bind off knitwise, taking care not to do so too tightly.

FINISHING

Weave in any loose ends, then block and steam gently. Using size 8 (5 mm) needles and with RS facing, pick up and knit 86 [93, 100] sts between the markers on one side edge. Bind off knitwise. Repeat on the other side edge. Fold the shrug in half with RS together so that the curved edges meet. Backstitch the seam from the cast-on edge to the the marker on the side edge. Repeat for the other seam from the bind-off edge.

Project 13: Sequined collar cape

Although chunky in appearance, this cape is very light-weight and is a good introduction to simple shaping techniques. Perfect for evening wear, the collar is knitted in garter stitch and subtly decorated with sequins and beads. The cape fastens with a large bow made of sheer ribbon edged with yarn.

before you start

MEASUREMENTS

Small [medium, large]
Width = 24½ [26¾, 29]"
(62 [68, 74] cm)
Length = 13½ [14, 15]"
(34 [36, 38] cm)

YARN

Bulky-weight yarn (56% wool, 20% viscose, 14% polyamide, 10% silk; 87 yds/80 m per 2 oz/50 g ball) x 5 [6, 6] balls (pink tweed)

BEADS AND NOTIONS

100 x 2 mm pink beads
100 x 8 mm pearl sequins
Two 38" (96 cm) lengths of 1½" (4 cm) wide sheer ribbon

NEEDLES

Size 10½ (6.5 mm); size 11 (7 mm)

GAUGE

14 sts x 16 rows = 4" (10 cm) in stockinette stitch using size 11 (7 mm) needles

ABBREVIATIONS

k—knit; k1f&b—knit into front and back of stitch; p—purl; RS—right side; st(s)—stitch(es); tbl—through back of loop; tog—together; WS—wrong side

BACK

Using size 11 (7 mm) needles, cast on 90 [100, 108] sts. Beginning at the bottom right of the cape chart on pages 88–89, work the back piece in stockinette stitch, placing the ribbing and shaping the sides and shoulders as indicated. Decrease at the beginning of a row by k2tog tbl; decrease at the end of a row by k2tog. When you reach the neck shaping (row 59 [63, 65]), bind off the required number of stitches at the beginning of the row knitwise, continue to the asterisk, then turn the work. Bind off the required number of stitches for the neck purlwise, complete the row, then bind off the remaining stitches knitwise. With RS facing, rejoin the yarn to the remaining stitches and complete as indicated on the chart.

RIGHT FRONT

Using size 11 (7 mm) needles, cast on 45 [50, 54] sts. Beginning at the center of the cape chart on pages 88–89 as indicated, work the right front piece in stockinette stitch, placing the ribbing and shaping the side and neck as indicated (decrease as instructed for the back). When the last row of chart has been completed, bind off the remaining stitches knitwise.

Pearl sequins topped with pink beads provide decoration on the textured collar without detracting from the subtle hues of the tweed yarn.

LEFT FRONT

Using size 11 (7 mm) needles, cast on 45 [50, 54] sts. Beginning at the bottom right of the cape chart on pages 88–89, work the left front piece in stockinette stitch, placing the ribbing and shaping the side and neck as indicated (decrease as instructed for the back). When the last row of chart has been completed, bind off the remaining stitches knitwise.

SEWING THE CAPE

Weave in any loose ends, then block and steam gently. Place the right front piece onto the back with RS together and cast-on edges aligned, then backstitch the seam. Repeat for the left front piece. Place markers in both the right and left front pieces on the neck edge where the shaping ends (row 45 [49, 51]).

COLLAR

Using size 10½ (6.5 mm) needles, cast on 3 [5, 6] sts. Beginning at the bottom right of the collar chart on pages 88–89, work the collar in garter stitch (knit every row), shaping the collar as indicated on the chart by k1f&b until row 52 has been completed. Place a marker at the end of this row. Work in garter stitch without any additional shaping until this straight section of the collar fits around the neck edge of the cape between the markers when slightly stretched. Return to row 53 of the chart and continue in garter stitch, shaping the collar as indicated by k2tog tbl. When the final row of the chart has been completed, bind off knitwise.

FINISHING

Position the narrow ends of the collar at the beginning of the neck shaping, with the RS of the collar facing the WS of the cape. Overcast in place. Using matching sewing thread, sew sequins onto the collar with a bead in the center of each one. Start at the narrow end of the collar with closely clustered sequins, spacing them more widely apart as you move upward. The precise number and placement of sequins and beads is up to you. Using a sewing machine, edge the ribbon with a line of yarn stitches and hem the ends. Sew a piece of ribbon at the opening edge on each side of the cape just below the collar.

> **NOTE: Cape back and front**
> On the cape chart, knit the complete chart for the back piece, following the outermost lines for the size you are making and ignoring the V shape in the center of the chart. The V-shaped lines indicate the shaping of the front pieces only, so follow the innermost lines when making the front pieces, starting where indicated on the chart.

Collar

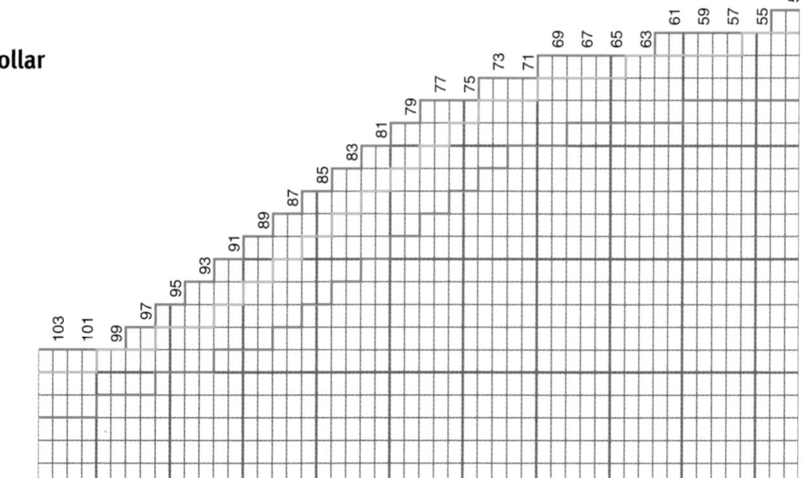

Cape

Begin here for right front

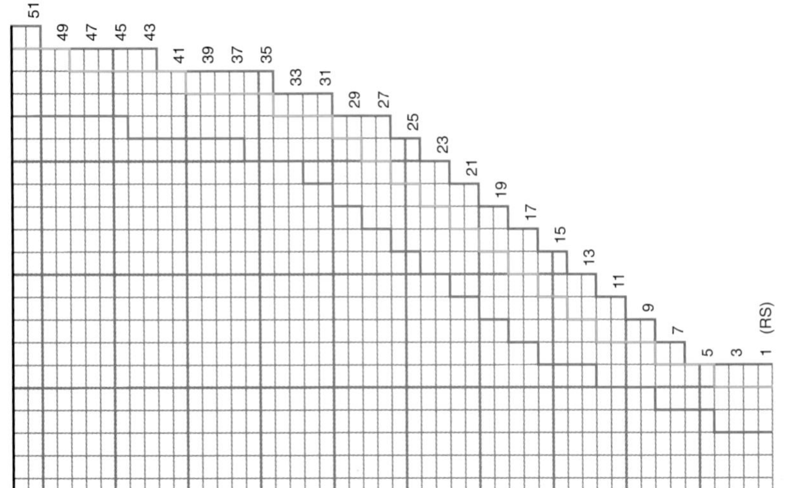

KEY (both charts)

- on cape: k on RS, p on WS; on collar: k on RS and WS
- • p on RS, k on WS
- ✱ place marker for neck shaping
- large
- medium
- small

NOTE: Following the charts

Each chart has been divided so that nothing is lost where the pages of the book join. Simply ignore the space between the two sections and work across each chart as if it were a single illustration.

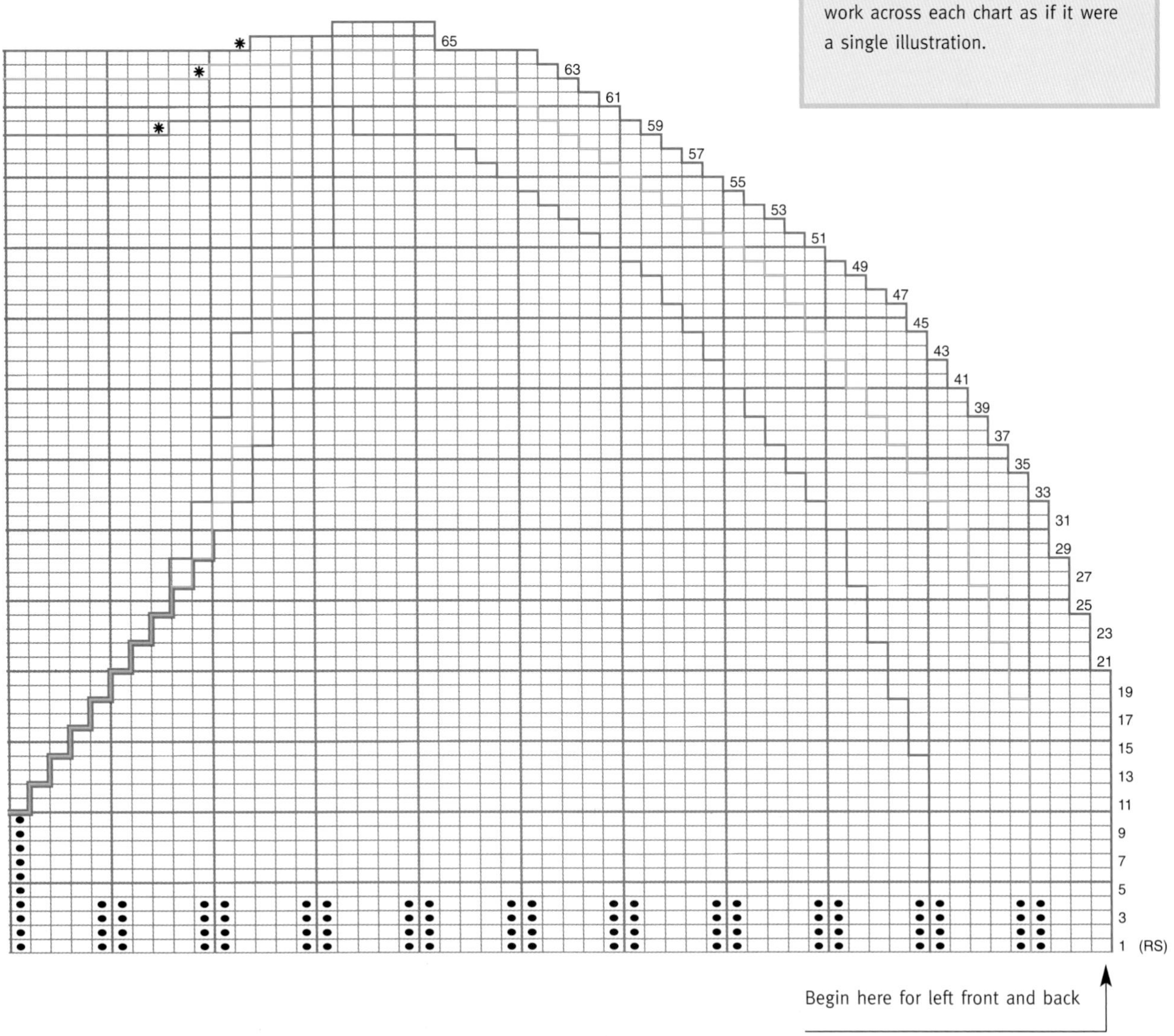

Begin here for left front and back

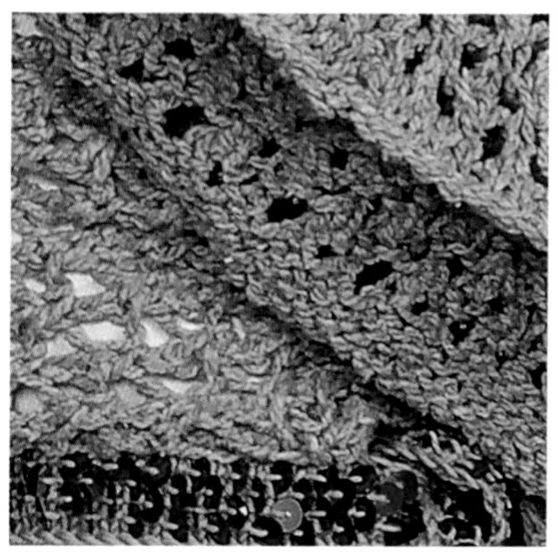

Project 14: Lacy hip-tie v-neck

This versatile top can be worn when relaxing at home or as a poncho-style top when going out for an evening. You can even take it to the beach to slip on if the weather gets a little cool. It is made from two basic rectangles, one with V-neck shaping that is very easy to do.

BACK

Using size 10½ (6.5 mm) needles and yarn A, cast on 77 [81, 85] sts.

Row 1 (RS): Knit.

Row 2: Purl.

Begin lace pattern as follows:

Row 3: K1, *yo, s2kpo, yo, k1, repeat from * to end.

Row 4: Purl.

Row 5: K2tog, yo, k1, *yo, s2kpo, yo, k1, repeat from * to last 2 sts, yo, k2tog.

Row 6: Purl.

Repeat rows 3–6 until a total of 184 [200, 216] rows have been worked.

Beginning with a knit row, work two rows in stockinette stitch.

Bind off knitwise.

FRONT

Using size 10½ (6.5 mm) needles and yarn A, cast on 77 [81, 85] sts.

Work as for rows 1–6 of back. Repeat rows 3–6 until 77 [83, 89] rows have been worked.

Shape the neck as follows, following the instructions for the appropriate size.

Neck shaping—small size

Row 78 (WS): Bind off 6 sts purlwise, purl to end (71 sts).

Row 79: K1, *yo, s2kpo, yo, k1, repeat from * to last 6 sts, knit to end.

Row 80: As row 78 (65 sts).

Row 81: K2tog, yo, k1, *yo, s2kpo, yo, k1, repeat from * to last 6 sts, knit to end.

Row 82: As row 78 (59 sts).

Row 83: As row 79.

Row 84: As row 78 (53 sts).

Row 85: As row 81.

Row 86: Bind off 5 sts purlwise, purl to end (48 sts).

Row 87: K1, *yo, s2kpo, yo, k1, repeat from * to last 3 sts, k3.

Row 88: Bind off 4 sts purlwise, purl to end (44 sts).

Row 89: K2tog, yo, k1, *yo, s2kpo, yo, k1, repeat from * to last 5 sts, knit to end.

Row 90: As row 88 (40 sts).

Row 91: As row 87.

Row 92: As row 88 (36 sts).

Row 93: K2tog, yo, k1, *yo, s2kpo, yo, k1, repeat from * to last st, k1.

Row 94: Cast on 4 sts, purl to end (40 sts).

Row 95: As row 87.

Row 96: As row 94 (44 sts).

before you start

MEASUREMENTS

Small [medium, large]

Width from cast-on to bind-off edge = 46 [49½, 53]" (117 [126, 135] cm)

Length from shoulder to hip = 22½ [23¼, 24]" (57 [59, 61] cm)

YARN

A Aran-weight yarn (70% silk, 30% cotton; approx. 118 yds/108 m per 2 oz/50 g ball) x 10 [12, 14] balls (green tweed)

B Light-weight yarn (100% cotton; approx. 137 yds/115 m per 2 oz/50 g ball) x 2 [3, 3] balls (green)

SEQUINS

1,800 x 8 mm green sequins

NEEDLES

Size 10½ (6.5 mm) straight needles; 1 yd (1 m) long size 5 (3.75 mm) circular needle

GAUGE

13 sts x 16 rows = 4" (10 cm) in lace pattern using size 10½ (6.5 mm) needles and yarn A

26 sts x 30 rows = 4" (10 cm) in sequined pattern using size 5 (3.75 mm) needle and yarn B

ABBREVIATIONS

k—knit; RS—right side; seq 1—place 1 sequin and slip 1 stitch purlwise; s2kpo—slip 2 sts purlwise, knit next st, pass slip sts over knitted st; st(s)—stitch(es); tog—together; WS—wrong side; yo—yarn over

The lacy panels are left unembellished so that the intricate lacy texture can be clearly seen, while the hip ties and V-neck are heavily sequined to emphasize the shaping of the top.

Row 97: K2tog, yo, k1, *yo, s2kpo, yo, k1, repeat from * to last st, k1.
Row 98: As row 94 (48 sts).
Row 99: As row 87.
Row 100: Cast on 5 sts, purl to end (53 sts).
Row 101: K2tog, yo, k1, *yo, s2kpo, yo, k1, repeat from * to last 2 sts, k2.
Row 102: Cast on 6 sts, purl to end (59 sts).
Row 103: K1, *yo, s2kpo, yo, k1, repeat from * to last 2 sts, k2.
Row 104: As row 102 (65 sts).
Row 105: As row 101.
Row 106: As row 102 (71 sts).
Row 107: As row 103.
Row 108: As row 102 (77 sts).
Row 109: As row 3.
Row 110: As row 4.
Continue in lace pattern as set by rows 3–6 until another 74 rows have been worked. Beginning with a knit row, work two rows in stockinette stitch.
Bind off knitwise.

Neck shaping—medium size

Row 84 (WS): Bind off 5 sts purlwise, purl to end (76 sts).
Row 85: K2tog, yo, k1, *yo, s2kpo, yo, k1, repeat from * to last 5 sts, knit to end.
Row 86: As row 84 (71 sts).
Row 87: K1, *yo, s2kpo, yo, k1, repeat from * to last 6 sts, knit to end.
Row 88: As row 84 (66 sts).
Row 89: K2tog, yo, k1, *yo, s2kpo, yo, k1, repeat from * to last 3 sts, knit to end.
Row 90: As row 84 (61 sts).
Row 91: K1, *yo, s2kpo, yo, k1, repeat from * to last 4 sts, knit to end.
Row 92: As row 84 (56 sts).
Row 93: As row 85.
Row 94: As row 84 (51 sts).
Row 95: K1, *yo, s2kpo, yo, k1, repeat from * to last 2 sts, k2.
Row 96: As row 84 (46 sts).
Row 97: As row 89.
Row 98: As row 84 (41 sts).
Row 99: K1, *yo, s2kpo, yo, k1, repeat from * to last 4 sts, knit to end.
Row 100: As row 84 (36 sts).
Row 101: K2tog, yo, k1, *yo, s2kpo, yo, k1, repeat from * to last st, k1.
Row 102: Cast on 5 sts, purl to end (41 sts).
Row 103: K1, *yo, s2kpo, yo, k1, repeat from * to end.
Row 104: As row 102 (46 sts).
Row 105: K2tog, yo, k1, *yo, s2kpo, yo, k1, repeat from * to last 3 sts, k3.
Row 106: As row 102 (51 sts).
Row 107: K1, *yo, s2kpo, yo, k1, repeat from * to last 2 sts, k2.
Row 108: As row 102 (56 sts).
Row 109: K2tog, yo, k1, *yo, s2kpo, yo, k1, repeat from * to last st, k1.
Row 110: As row 102 (61 sts).
Row 111: As row 103.
Row 112: As row 102 (66 sts).
Row 113: K2tog, yo, k1, *yo, s2kpo, yo, k1, repeat from * to last 2 sts, k2.
Row 114: As row 102 (71 sts).
Row 115: K1, *yo, s2kpo, yo, k1, repeat from * to last 2 sts, k2.
Row 116: As row 102 (76 sts).
Row 117: K2tog, yo, k1, *yo, s2kpo, yo, k1, repeat from * to last st, k1.
Row 118: As row 102 (81 sts).
Continue in pattern as set by rows 3–6 until another 82 rows have been worked. Beginning with a knit row, work two rows in stockinette stitch.
Bind off purlwise.

Neck shaping—large size

Row 90 (WS): Bind off 5 sts purlwise, purl to end (80 sts).
Row 91: K1, *yo, s2kpo, yo, k1, repeat from * to last 3 sts, knit to end.
Row 92: As row 90 (75 sts).
Row 93: K2tog, yo, k1, *yo, s2kpo, yo, k1, repeat from * to last 5 sts, knit to end.
Row 94: As row 90 (70 sts).
Row 95: K1, *yo, s2kpo, yo, k1, repeat from * to last 5 sts, knit to end.
Row 96: As row 90 (65 sts).
Row 97: K2tog, yo, k1, *yo, s2kpo, yo, k1, repeat from * to last 6 sts, knit to end.
Row 98: As row 90 (60 sts).
Row 99: As row 91.
Row 100: Bind off 4 sts purlwise, purl to end (56 sts).
Row 101: K2tog, yo, k1, *yo, s2kpo, yo, k1, repeat from * to last 5 sts, knit to end.
Row 102: As row 100 (52 sts).
Row 103: As row 91.
Row 104: As row 100 (48 sts).
Row 105: As row 93.
Row 106: As row 100 (44 sts).
Row 107: As row 91.
Row 108: As row 100 (40 sts).
Row 109: K2tog, yo, k1, *yo, s2kpo, yo, k1, repeat from * to last st, k1.
Row 110: Cast on 4 sts, purl to end (44 sts).
Row 111: K1, *yo, s2kpo, yo, k1, repeat from * to last 3 sts, knit to end.
Row 112: As row 110 (48 sts).
Row 113: As row 109.
Row 114: As row 110 (52 sts).
Row 115: As row 111.
Row 116: As row 110 (56 sts).
Row 117: As row 109.
Row 118: As row 110 (60 sts).
Row 119: As row 111.
Row 120: Cast on 5 sts, purl to end (65 sts).
Row 121: K2tog, yo, k1, *yo, s2kpo, yo, k1, repeat from * to last 2 sts, k2.
Row 122: As row 120 (70 sts).
Row 123: K1, *yo, s2kpo, yo, k1, repeat from * to last st, k1.
Row 124: As row 120 (75 sts).
Row 125: K2tog, yo, k1, * yo, s2kpo, yo, k1, repeat from * to end.
Row 126: As row 120 (80 sts).
Row 127: As row 111.
Row 128: As row 120 (85 sts).
Row 129: K2tog, yo, k1, *yo, s2kpo, yo, k1, repeat from * to last 2 sts, yo, k2tog.
Row 130: Purl.
Continue in lace pattern as set by rows 3–6 until another 88 rows have been worked. Beginning with a knit row, work two rows in stockinette stitch.
Bind off knitwise.

HIP TIES (make 2)

Thread 500 sequins onto yarn B in batches of 100 at a time, breaking off and rejoining the yarn to thread on more sequins as necessary. Using a size 5 (3.75 mm) circular needle and yarn B, cast on 241 sts. Work back and forth as if using two needles.

Row 1 (RS): Knit.
Row 2: K1, purl to last st, k1.
Row 3: (K1, seq 1) to last st, k1.
Row 4: K1, purl to last st, k1.
Row 5: K2, (seq 1, k1) to last st, k1.
Row 6: K1, purl to last st, k1.
Rows 7–10: Repeat rows 3–6 once.
Bind off knitwise.

NECK TRIM

Thread 800 sequins onto yarn B in batches of 100 as before. Using a size 5 (3.75 mm) circular needle and yarn B, cast on 241 sts. Work back and forth as if using two needles.

Row 1 (RS): Knit.
Row 2: K1, purl to last st, k1.
Row 3: K2tog, (seq 1, k1) to last 3 sts, seq 1, k2tog.
Row 4: K1, purl to last st, k1.
Rows 5–14: Repeat rows 3–4 five times.
Bind off knitwise.

FINISHING

Weave in any loose ends, then block and steam gently. Sewing all seams using a fine backstitch, place the panels RS together and start by sewing the shoulder seams. Beginning and ending at center front and with RS together, sew the neck trim in place using yarn B. With RS together, sew the hip ties together at one end. Position the joined seam of the ties 13½ [14, 15]" (34 [36, 38] cm) from the cast-on or bind-off edge and sew to the bottom edge of the front and back pieces. Stop sewing an equal distance from the other edge of the front and back pieces, allowing the ties to hang loose for tying the top around the hips.

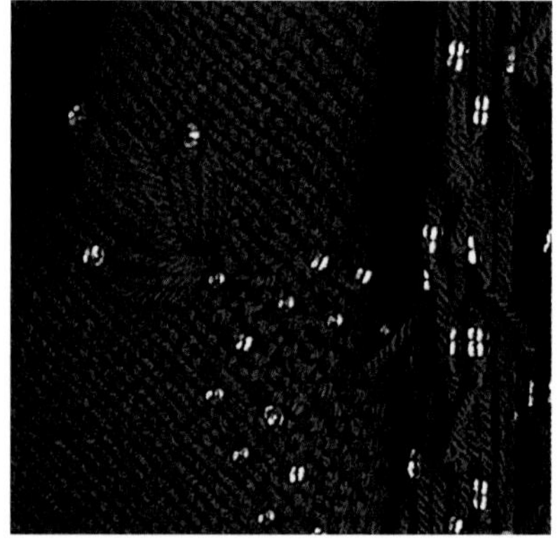

Project 15: Luxurious beaded wrap

This wrap is knitted in a merino wool/cashmere blend yarn. It is so beautifully soft that the texture and decoration have been deliberately played down on the body of the wrap, but an extravagant beaded fringe is added to provide drama. The chain stitch motifs add to the subtle decoration, while the fringe is shaped to echo the seed stitch texture at the ends of the wrap.

MAIN PANEL

Thread 141 beads onto one end of yarn, alternating 1 clear bead and 1 purple bead. Using size 7 (4.5 mm) needles and two ends of yarn together (one beaded, one plain), cast on 93 sts. Beginning at the bottom right of chart A on page 97, work the first end of the wrap, placing the seed stitch pattern and beads as indicated. When the last row of chart A has been completed, continue in stockinette stitch, beginning with a knit row and keeping the edge stitches as set in chart A until the wrap measures 72" (183 cm) long, ending with RS facing for next row. Break off the yarn and thread 141 beads onto the yarn, alternating colors as before. Rejoin the doubled yarn to the wrap and, beginning at the bottom right of chart B on page 97, work the 50 rows as indicated. When the last row of chart B has been completed, bind off knitwise.

FINISHING

Weave in any loose ends, then block and steam gently. Using four strands of yarn together, embroider chain stitch motifs on the tips of the seed stitch peaks (see page 31). Each motif is composed of three chain stitches. The central chain stitch should extend 10 rows straight up from the seed stitch peak; each side chain stitch should extend 5 rows upward and 3 stitches outward. Sew a clear bead at the tip of each chain stitch.

FRINGE

Add a beaded tassel fringe along each end of the wrap, using the yarn doubled for each tassel. Start with the lamp bead tassels. These beads are heavy so they have not been used all the way across the edge. There are symbols under chart A and above chart B to help with placing these beads. Where there is just one lamp bead tassel (below the lower points of the V), the tassel should be 3¼" (8 cm) long; where there are two lamp bead tassels (below the highest peaks of the V), each tassel should be 6½" (16 cm) long. In both cases, thread both strands of yarn through one lamp bead at one end of the tassel, and both strands of yarn through two small clear beads at the opposite end of the tassel. Secure the beads in place with a knot. Once the lamp bead tassels have been placed, fill in the gaps with tassels beaded at each end with two clear beads, lengthening and shortening the tassels as appropriate across the edge to echo the zigzag of the seed stitch texture.

before you start

MEASUREMENTS
19½" (50 cm) wide x 79" (200 cm) long excluding fringe

YARN
Sport-weight yarn (57% merino, 33% microfiber, 10% cashmere; approx. 197 yds/180 m per 2 oz/50 g ball) x 15 balls (purple)
Yarn is used doubled throughout

BEADS
300 x 3 mm gold-lined clear beads
150 x 3 mm iridescent purple beads
32 x 20 mm long gold-and-mauve drop-shaped lamp beads

NEEDLES
Size 7 (4.5 mm)

GAUGE
19 sts x 29 rows = 4" (10 cm) in stockinette stitch using size 7 (4.5 mm) needles and yarn doubled

ABBREVIATIONS
bead 1—place 1 bead and slip 1 stitch purlwise; k—knit; p—purl; RS—right side; st(s)—stitch(es); WS—wrong side

This gorgeous wrap is fringed with tassels that echo the shape of the patterned ends, and both are emphasized with beads.

New skills/tassel fringe

Start by cutting pieces of yarn twice the required finished length.

1 With the right side of the knitting facing you, insert a crochet hook from the front of the work into the first stitch one row in from the edge.

2 Fold a length of yarn in half and pull it halfway through to the front of the work. If a crochet hook is not suitable, such as when adding tassels to the center of a flower corsage, thread the folded end of yarn through a blunt-ended needle and use this to pull it through.

3 Insert the ends of the yarn through the folded loop and pull tight. Continue inserting tassels into each stitch along the edge of the knitting, or where required.

KEY

- ☐ k on RS, p on WS
- ⊡ p on RS, k on RS
- ◉ bead 1
- ▨ work stockinette stitch until wrap measures 72" (183 cm)
- ◉ place lamp-bead tassel during finishing

Chart B

Chart A

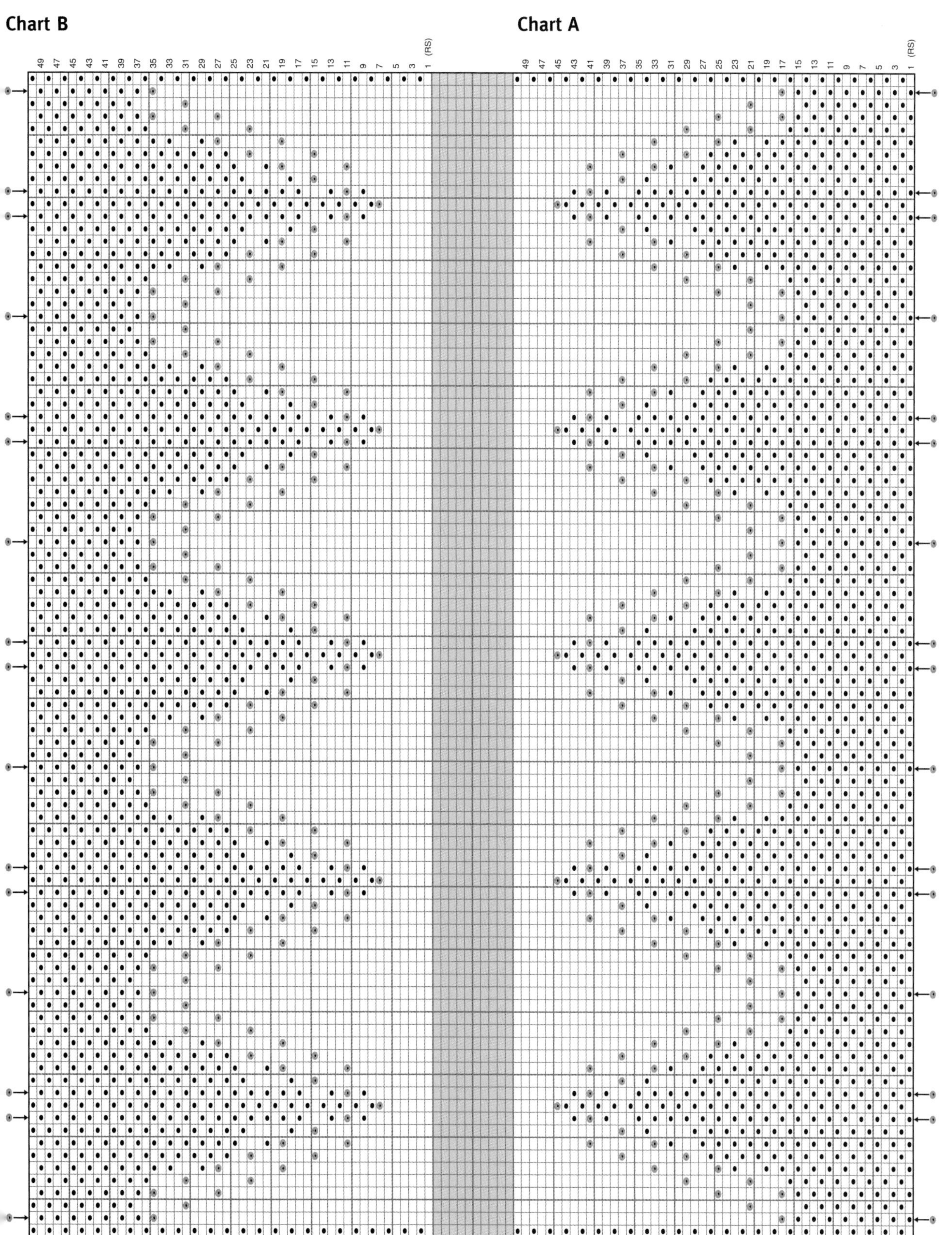

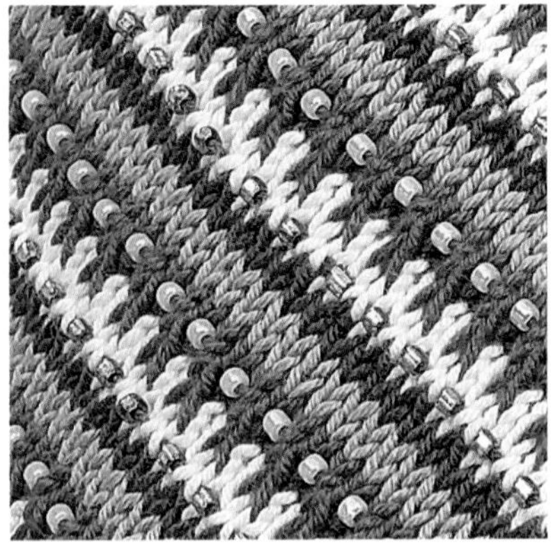

Project 16: Optic-striped pillow

This pillow knitted in a DK-weight wool/cotton blend yarn is much simpler than it may first appear. The front is knitted in four triangular sections that are worked individually and then sewn together to form the square. The back is knitted in one color and finished with a shell button fastening. You can create a variety of looks simply by changing the color scheme of the stripes.

before you start

MEASUREMENTS
14" (36 cm) square

YARN
DK-weight yarn (50% wool, 50% cotton; approx. 123 yds/113 m per 2 oz/50 g ball) in 4 colors:
A Lilac x 1 ball
B Purple x 1 ball
C Cream x 1 ball
D Blue x 2 balls

BEADS AND NOTIONS
390 x 3 mm blue beads
450 x 3 mm white beads
14" (36 cm) square pillow form
Five ⅞" (22 mm) diameter gray shell buttons

NEEDLES
Size 5 (3.75 mm)

GAUGE
24 sts x 32 rows = 4" (10 cm) in beaded pattern using size 5 (3.75 mm) needles
24 sts x 30 rows = 4" (10 cm) in stockinette stitch using size 5 (3.75 mm) needles

ABBREVIATIONS
bead 1—place 1 bead and slip 1 stitch purlwise; k—knit; p—purl; RS—right side; sl 1—slip 1 stitch knitwise or purlwise as indicated; st(s)—stitch(es); tog—together; WS—wrong side

FRONT (make 4)

Thread 101 blue beads onto yarn D and 87 white beads onto yarn B. Using size 5 (3.75 mm) needles and yarn A, cast on 61 sts and work from the chart on page 100, beginning at the bottom right and placing beads and decreasing where indicated. Decrease on a RS row using k2tog; decrease on a WS row using p2tog. Carry the yarns not in use up the side of the work. When the last row of the chart has been completed, bind off the remaining stitches purlwise.

UPPER BACK

Using size 5 (3.75 mm) needles and yarn C, cast on 85 sts. Break off yarn C and join yarn D.
Rows 1–4: Beginning with a knit row, work four rows in stockinette stitch.
Row 5 (buttonhole row): K11, *bind off 3 sts knitwise, k12, repeat from * until 4 buttonholes have been made, bind off 3 sts knitwise, k11.
Row 6: P11, *cast on 3 sts, p12, repeat from * until four buttonholes have been completed, cast on 3 sts, p11.
Beginning with a knit row, continue in stockinette stitch until work measures 5½" (14 cm) from cast-on edge.
Bind off knitwise.

LOWER BACK

Using size 5 (3.75 mm) needles and yarn D, cast on 85 sts. Beginning with a knit row, work in stockinette stitch until lower back measures 9" (23 cm).
Break off yarn D.
Bind off knitwise using yarn A.

FINISHING

Weave in any loose ends, then block and steam gently. With RS uppermost, lay out the four front sections so that they form a square with the decreased edges outermost. With RS together, backstitch the four pieces together, one seam at a time. Place the upper back and front RS together, with the bind-off edge of the upper back aligned with the top edge of the front. Backstitch the top seam. Place the lower back and front RS together, with the cast-on edge of the lower back aligned with the bottom edge of the front.

Tones of blue and purple make a pretty striped pattern, but you could use bright jazzy shades if you prefer, or even vary the colors used in each triangular section.

New skills/carrying yarn up side of work

When using multiple yarns to knit horizontal stripes, you can break off and join the yarns for each stripe, or carry them up the side of the work when not in use. The latter method reduces the number of yarn ends that need to be woven in when you have finished the project. Avoid pulling the yarns too tightly when carrying them up the side because this can cause the edge to distort.

1 After completing the first stripe, drop that color. Pick up the new color from under the old one, insert the right needle into the first stitch, and work the next stripe with the new color.

2 For stripes with more than two rows in one color, catch in the unused yarn on every other row by picking up the current yarn from under the unused yarn as you begin the new row.

Backstitch the bottom seam. Making sure that upper back will be outermost when you turn the pillow RS out, and that it overlaps the lower back by ⅞" (2 cm), join the remaining two side seams. Turn the pillow cover RS out and sew the buttons to the lower back to correspond with the buttonholes. Insert the pillow form and fasten the buttons.

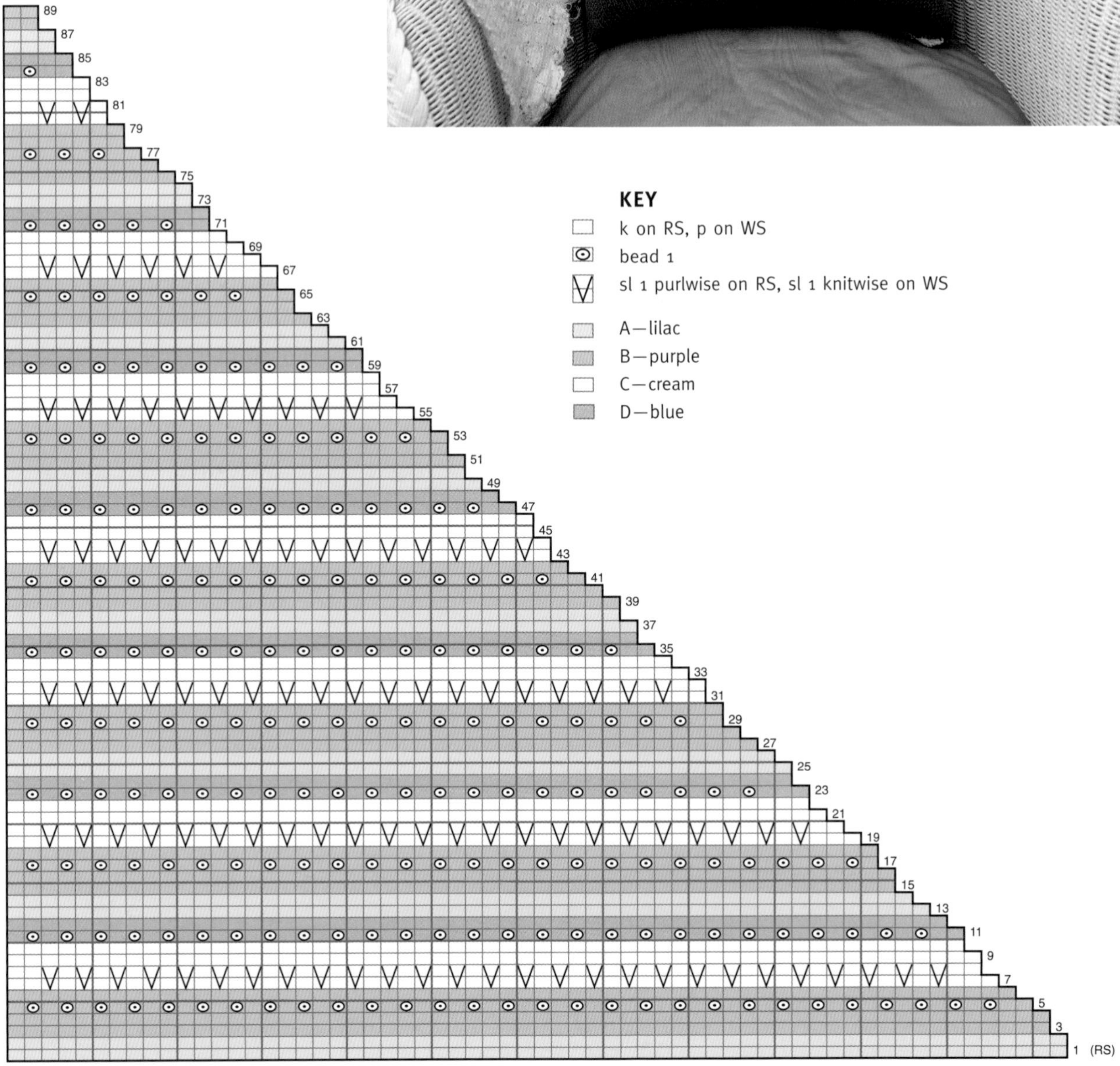

1 (RS) 3 5 7 9 11 13 15 17 19 21 23 25 27 29 31 33 35 37 39 41 43 45 47 49 51 53 55 57 59 61 63 65 67 69 71 73 75 77 79 81 83 85 87 89

KEY

- k on RS, p on WS
- bead 1
- sl 1 purlwise on RS, sl 1 knitwise on WS
- A—lilac
- B—purple
- C—cream
- D—blue

Project 17: Floral striped bolster

Tendrils created using a textured stitch pattern are embellished with beads to create a floral design on this pretty bolster. Shiny metallic yarns are used to highlight the stripes across the panels, and at intervals on the side sections. The bolster is closed using i-cords, which are very easy to make.

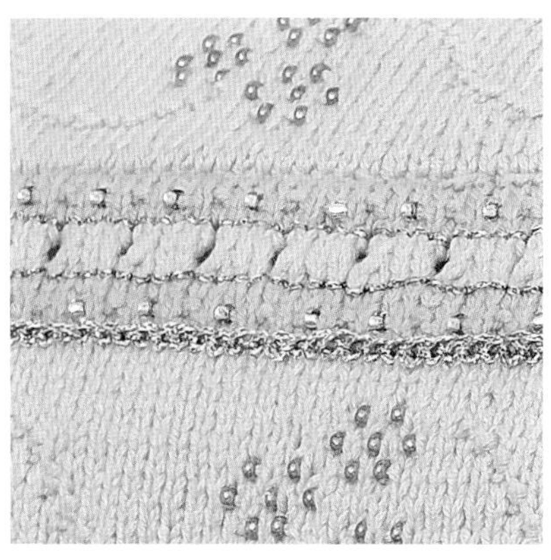

New skills/i-cord

I-cord is very easy to make using double-pointed needles. If you find that you work a lot with i-cords, use a knitting mill—it saves time.

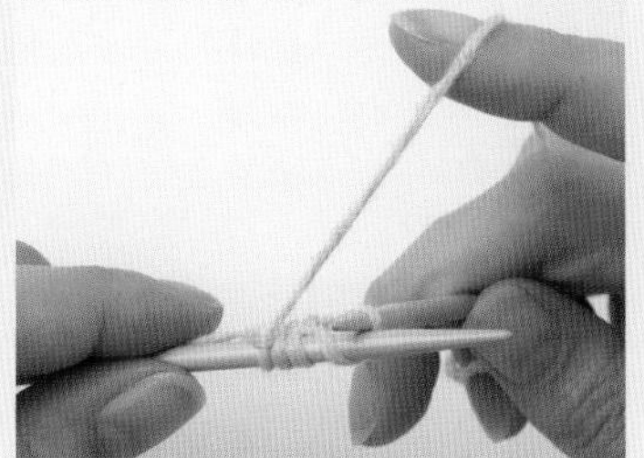

1 Cast on the required number of stitches and knit one row. Slide the stitches along the right needle from the left to the right tip. Transfer this needle to your left hand, so that the working end of the yarn is coming from the bottom stitch.

2 Knit the next row, pulling the yarn tightly across the back of the stitches as you do so. Repeat until the cord is the required length. Cut the yarn, thread it through all the stitches, and fasten securely.

MAIN PANEL

Thread 100 pink beads onto yarn A and 100 silver beads onto yarn B. Using size 7 (4.5 mm) needles and yarn A, cast on 100 sts. Starting at the bottom right of the chart on page 102, work four repeats of pattern, changing colors and placing beads and lace holes as indicated. Break off and rejoin the yarns to thread on more beads as necessary. When the last row of the final repeat has been worked, bind off knitwise using yarn B.

SIDES (work 2)

Thread 150 silver beads onto yarn B. Using size 7 (4.5 mm) needles and with RS facing, pick up and knit 160 sts along one side edge of the main panel.

Row 1 (WS): Purl.

Row 2 (RS): Knit.

Row 3: Purl.

Row 4: P2, *bead 1, k1, p1, k1, repeat from * to end.

before you start

MEASUREMENTS
8¾" (22 cm) diameter x 17¾" (45 cm) long excluding side gathers

YARN
DK-weight yarn (75% cotton, 25% microfiber; approx. 175 yds/160 m per 2 oz/50 g ball) in 2 colors:
A Pink x 4 balls
B Gray x 3 balls
Light-weight yarn (80% viscose, 20% polyester; approx. 103 yds/95 m per 1 oz/25 g ball) in 2 colors:
C Metallic pink x 1 ball
D Metallic gray x 2 balls

BEADS AND NOTIONS
700 x 3 mm pink beads
900 x 3 mm silver beads
8¾" (22 cm) diameter x 17¾" (45 cm) long bolster pillow form

NEEDLES
Size 7 (4.5 mm) straight needles; two size 6 (4 mm) double-pointed needles or a knitting mill

GAUGE
22 sts x 30 rows = 4" (10 cm) in stockinette stitch using size 7 (4.5 mm) needles

ABBREVIATIONS
bead 1—place 1 bead and slip 1 stitch purlwise; k—knit; p—purl; RS—right side; st(s)—stitch(es); tog—together; WS—wrong side; yo—yarn over

New skills/pekinese stitch

Also known as Chinese stitch, this embroidery stitch is composed of interlaced backstitches to produce a braid effect.

1 Work a row of backstitches (see page 38). Starting at the left edge, thread the yarn upward under the second backstitch along, then downward under the first backstitch. Do not catch in the knitted fabric beneath the backstitches.

2 Continue lacing the yarn under the backstitches, keeping the loops even.

3 You can leave the laced yarn as it is, or pull it tighter to eliminate the loops above the backstitches to produce a finer braid effect.

Row 5: Purl.

Without breaking off yarn B, join yarn A. Work rows 6–9 using yarn A, carrying yarn B loosely up the side of the work.

Row 6: Knit.

Row 7: Purl.

Row 8: (K2, k2tog, yo) to last 2 sts, k2.

Row 9: Purl.

Carrying the yarn not in use up the side of the work, repeat the pattern as set by rows 2–9, until another five repeats of stripe pattern have been completed.

KEY

- k on RS, p on WS
- p on RS, k on WS
- bead 1
- k2tog
- yo
- A—pink
- B—gray

Break off both yarns. Bind off knitwise using yarn C.

Repeat along the other side edge of the main panel.

FINISHING

Weave in any loose ends, then block and steam gently. On the main panel, use yarn D to sew a line of backstitches along the outer edges of each pair of yarn B stripes. Using yarn C, work pekinese stitch into the lines of backstitch. On the side panels, beginning with the yarn B stripe farthest from the bind-off edge, use yarn D to sew a line of backstitches in the last knitted row. Repeat for every alternate yarn B stripe. With RS together, form into a cylinder shape, with cast-on edge to bind-off edge of the main panel, and matching the stripes on the side panels. Backstitch the seam. Turn RS out. Using size 6 (4 mm) double-pointed needles and yarn A, cast on 4 sts and make two 4' (1.2 m) long i-cords to use as ties. Finish off both ends of each tie by adding a 2½" (6 cm) long tassel. Each tassel should have eight strands (four wraps around the cardboard); thread two leftover beads onto each strand, knotting them securely in place. Thread a tie through the third row of lace holes from the bind-off edge of each side panel. Pull the ties to gather the sides together and fasten with a bow.

This bolster pillow is perfect for a feminine bedroom or a light and airy sunroom. Adapt the color scheme to suit your decor and personal taste.

New skills

Tassels, see page 43

Carrying yarn up side of work, see page 99

Project 18: Floral summer throw

Knitted in DK-weight cotton yarn, this throw is made up of five scarf-sized panels joined together to create a riot of color. The solid-colored panels feature subtle beading and purl-textured rectangles, and are contrasted with jazzy striped panels in between. The flowers are knitted separately, embellished with beads, and sewn onto the throw at the end.

BEADED PANELS (make 3)

Thread the pink beads onto yarn A in batches of 100 at a time, breaking off and rejoining the yarn to thread on more beads as necessary. Using size 6 (4 mm) needles and yarn A, cast on 39 sts.

Row 1 (RS): (K1, p1) to last st, k1.
Rows 2–4: Repeat row 1 three times.
Rows 5–60: Beginning at the bottom right of chart A on page 106, work the panel, placing purl stitches and beads as indicated until the last row of the chart has been completed.
Rows 61–396: Repeat rows 5–60 six times.
Rows 397–424: Repeat rows 5–32 once.
Rows 425–428: Repeat row 1 four times.
Bind off in pattern.
Make two more panels in the same way, using yarn B with purple beads for one, and yarn C with green beads for the other.

STRIPED PANELS (make 2)

Using size 6 (4 mm) needles and yarn D, cast on 39 sts.

Rows 1–48: Starting at the bottom right of chart B on page 107, work the panel, placing purl stitches and changing colors as indicated until the last row of the chart has been completed.
Rows 49–384: Repeat rows 1–48 seven times.
Rows 385–418: Repeat rows 1–30 once.
Rows 419–422: Repeat rows 1–4 once.
Bind off in pattern.
Make a second striped panel in the same way, but follow chart C.

SEWING THE PANELS

Weave in any loose ends, then block and steam gently. With RS together, place the yarn A beaded panel on top of the chart B striped panel. Making sure that the cast-on and bind-off edges align, sew the panels together down the left side edge. Open flat and steam the seam open on WS. With RS together, sew the yarn B beaded panel to the other side edge of the chart B striped panel. Steam the seam open as before. Repeat this process to add the yarn C beaded panel and then the chart C striped panel. All the following instructions refer to the yarn A beaded panel as the left side of the throw.

FLOWERS—1ST COLUMN (make 4)

Using size 6 (4 mm) needles and yarn F, cast on 55 sts. Break off yarn F and join yarn D.

Row 1 (RS): *K1, yo, p3, p3tog, p3, yo, k1, repeat from * to end.
Row 2: Purl.
Row 3: *K1, yo, k3, k3tog, k3, yo, k1, repeat from * to end.
Row 4: Purl.
Row 5: As row 3.

before you start

MEASUREMENTS

38½" (98 cm) wide x
60" (152 cm) long

YARN

DK-weight yarn (100% cotton; approx. 93 yds/85 m per 2 oz/50 g ball) in 8 colors:

A Orange x 5 balls
B Pink x 6 balls
C Red x 6 balls
D Cream x 6 balls
E Purple x 2 balls
F Yellow x 2 balls
G Green x 2 balls
H Aqua x 2 balls

BEADS AND NOTIONS

520 x 3 mm red beads
480 x 3 mm purple beads
550 x 3 mm green beads

NEEDLES

Size 6 (4 mm)

GAUGE

20 sts x 28 rows = 4" (10 cm) in stockinette stitch using size 6 (4 mm) needles

ABBREVIATIONS

bead 1—place 1 bead and slip 1 stitch purlwise; k—knit; p—purl; RS—right side; st(s)—stitch(es); tog—together; WS—wrong side; yo—yarn over

Stripes are the theme of this throw. It is made from five panels joined together to create large vertical stripes, while two of the panels are striped horizontally. Even the flowers have a striped design.

Row 6: Purl.
Break off yarn D and join yarn B.
Row 7: K2tog to last st, k1 (28 sts).
Row 8: P2tog to end (14 sts).
Break off yarn B and draw tightly through remaining 14 sts to fasten off.
Cut four 4" (10 cm) strands of yarn F and attach them to the center of the flower in the same way as you would attach a tassel fringe. Thread three purple beads onto each strand of the tassels and knot to secure.
Sew the flowers down the left edge of the throw, positioning the first and last flowers 8" (20 cm) from the cast-on and bind-off edges, and the remaining two flowers evenly spaced between.

FLOWERS—2ND COLUMN (make 5)

Make another five flowers, but cast on using yarn D, then change to yarn C to work rows 1–6. Change to yarn F for rows 7–8. Make the tassel centers using yarn D and green beads. Sew the flowers along the first seam along from the left edge of the throw, positioning the first and last flowers on the cast-on and bind-off edges, with the remaining three flowers evenly spaced between.

FLOWERS—3RD COLUMN (make 4)

Make another four flowers, but cast on using yarn E, then change to yarn F to work rows 1–6. Change to yarn C for rows 7–8. Make the tassel centers using yarn G and red beads. Sew the flowers along the next seam along from the left edge of the throw, matching the position of the first column of flowers.

FLOWERS—4TH COLUMN (make 5)

Make another five flowers, but cast on using yarn C, then change to yarn D to work rows 1–6. Change to yarn B for rows 7–8. Make the tassel centers using yarn A and green beads. Sew the flowers along the next seam along from the left edge of the throw, matching the position of the second column of flowers.

Chart A

KEY (chart A)

- □ k on RS, p on WS
- ⊡ p on RS, k on WS
- ⊙ bead 1

Chart B

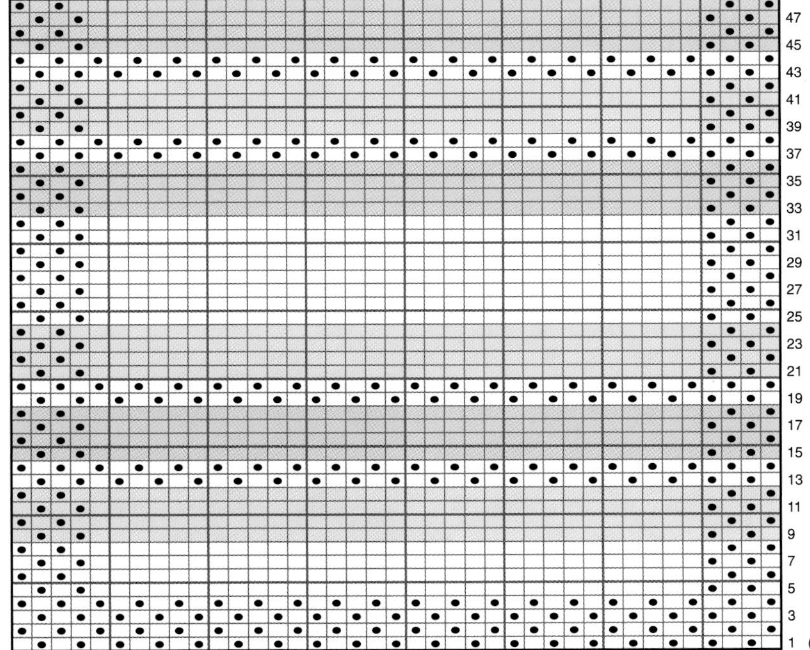

KEY (chart B)

- k on RS, p on WS
- p on RS, k on WS
- D—cream
- G—green
- H—aqua

KEY (chart C)

- k on RS, p on WS
- p on RS, k on WS
- D—cream
- E—purple
- F—yellow

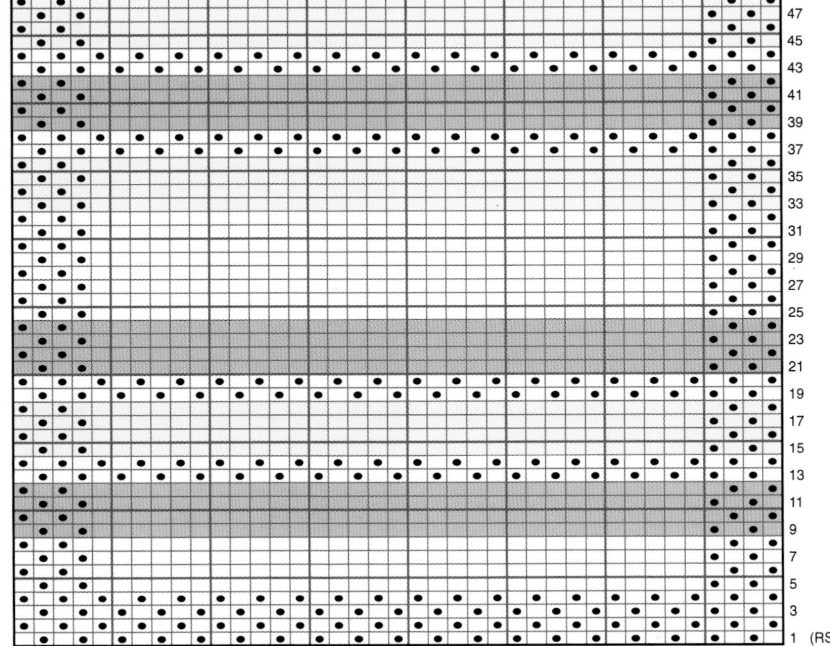

Chart C

FLOWERS—5TH COLUMN (make 4)

Make another four flowers, but cast on using yarn H, then change to yarn A to work rows 1–6. Change to yarn B for rows 7–8. Make the tassel centers using yarn B and purple beads. Sew the flowers along the next seam along from the left edge of the throw, matching the position of the first column of flowers.

FLOWERS—6TH COLUMN (make 5)

Make another five flowers, but cast on using yarn G, then change to yarn B to work rows 1–6. Change to yarn A for rows 7–8. Make the tassel centers using yarn H and red beads. Sew the flowers along the next seam along from the left edge of the throw, matching the position of the second column of flowers.

New skills

Carrying yarn up side of work, see page 99

Tassel fringe, see page 96

Project 19: Jeweled scented sachets

These scented sachets were inspired by the beautiful decoration of Fabergé eggs. With two very different color schemes—one rich and spicy, the other delicate and pastel—they each combine beads and sequins to create sweet-smelling projects that would make perfect gifts.

PASTEL SACHET FRONT

Thread 80 silver beads onto yarn A. Using size 5 (3.75 mm) needles and yarn A, cast on 23 sts. Beginning at the bottom right of the chart on page 110, work the sachet front, placing beads as indicated. When the last row of the chart has been completed, bind off knitwise.

PASTEL SACHET BACK

Thread 15 pearl sequins onto yarn B. Using size 5 (3.75 mm) needles and yarn B, cast on 23 sts. Beginning at the bottom right of the chart on page 110, work the sachet back, placing sequins and lace holes as indicated. When the last row of the chart has been completed, bind off knitwise.

SPICY SACHET FRONT

Thread 63 copper sequins onto yarn C. Using size 5 (3.75 mm) needles and

before you start

MEASUREMENTS
4" (10 cm) wide x 5⅛" (13 cm) long

YARN
Light-weight yarn (100% cotton; approx. 137 yds/115 m per 2 oz/50 g ball) in 4 colors:
A Lavender x 1 ball (pastel sachet)
B Lime x 1 ball (pastel sachet)
C Red x 1 ball (spicy sachet)
D Olive x 1 ball (spicy sachet)

BEADS AND NOTIONS
80 x 2 mm silver beads, 15 x 8 mm pearl sequins, and 15 x 10 mm pink teardrop beads for pastel sachet
63 x 8 mm copper holographic sequins, 53 x 8 mm red holographic sequins, and 14 x 10 mm green teardrop beads for spicy sachet
1 oz (30 g) dried lavender per sachet
Four 4 x 5⅛" (10 x 13 cm) pieces of sheer fabric, such as muslin

NEEDLES
Size 5 (3.75 mm)

GAUGE
23 sts x 32 rows = 4" (10 cm) in stockinette stitch using size 5 (3.75 mm) needles

ABBREVIATIONS
bead 1—place 1 bead and slip 1 stitch purlwise; k—knit; p—purl; RS—right side; seq 1—place 1 sequin and slip 1 stitch purlwise; st(s)—stitch(es); tog—together; WS—wrong side; yo—yarn over

yarn C, cast on 23 sts. Beginning at the bottom right of the chart on page 110, work the sachet front, placing sequins as indicated. When the last row of the chart has been completed, bind off knitwise.

SPICY SACHET BACK

Thread 53 red sequins onto yarn D. Using size 5 (3.75 mm) needles and yarn D, cast on 23 sts. Beginning at the bottom right of the chart on page 110, work the sachet back, placing sequins and lace holes as indicated. When the last row of the chart has been completed, bind off knitwise.

FINISHING

Weave in any loose ends, then block and steam gently. Sew a piece of sheer fabric to the WS of all pieces using matching sewing thread, taking care that the

The front of the spicy sachet (left) is embellished with drop beads and a mass of brilliant sequins, while the front of the pastel sachet (right) has a more subtle beaded diamond design.

stitching does not show on the RS of the knitting. On the pastel sachet front, sew a pink teardrop bead onto the purl stitches where the diamonds meet (see chart) using matching thread. On the spicy sachet front, sew a green teardrop bead onto the purl stitches (see chart) using matching thread. With RS of front and back pieces together, backstitch around three sides of each sachet. Turn the sachets RS out and fill each with lavender. Sew the remaining seams on the outside with matching yarn.

Pastel sachet front

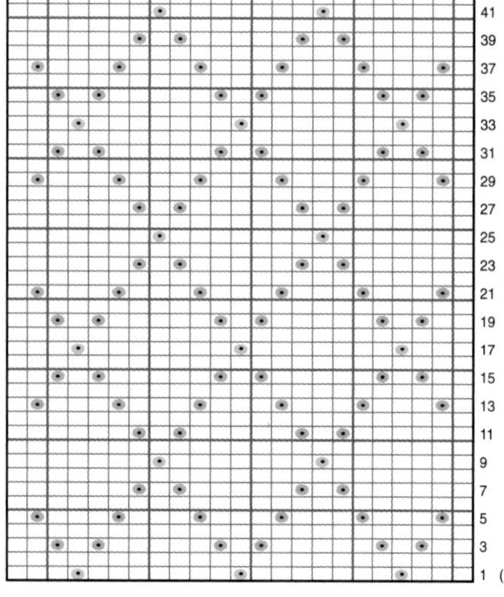

Pastel sachet back

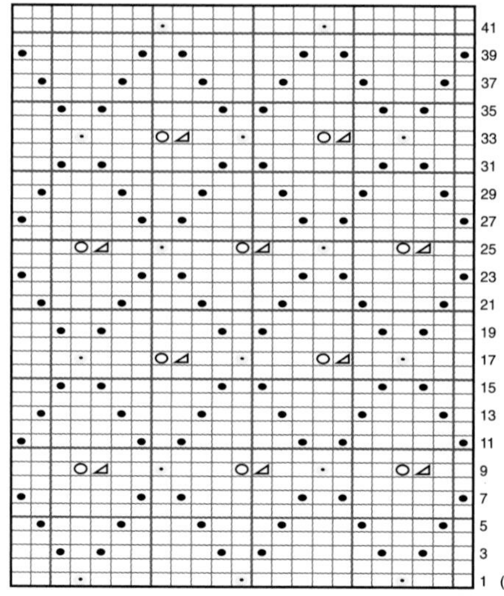

KEY (pastel sachet)

- k on RS, p on WS
- p on RS, k on WS
- p on RS, then sew pink teardrop bead to st during finishing
- bead 1—silver
- seq 1—pearl
- k2tog
- yo

Spicy sachet front

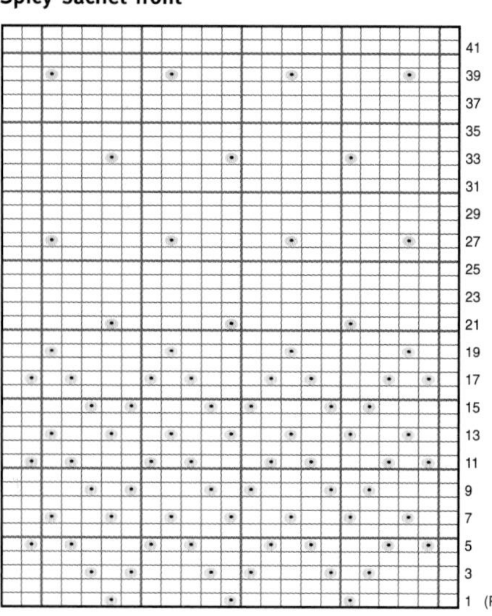

Spicy sachet back

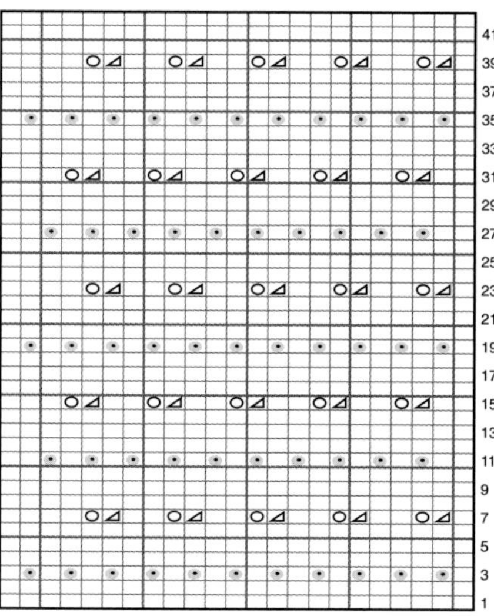

KEY (spicy sachet)

- k on RS, p on WS
- p on RS, then sew green teardrop bead to st during finishing
- seq 1—copper
- seq 1—red
- k2tog
- yo

Project 20: Circular suede pillow

This pillow is knitted using suede thong. This can be quite firm to work with, so the stitch texture and shaping have deliberately been kept simple. The large beads are sewn to the front afterward rather than knitted in, and are also used to fasten the pillow on the back.

before you start

MEASUREMENTS
16" (40 cm) diameter

YARN
136 yds (125 m) of ¼" (5 mm) wide natural-colored flat suede thong

BEADS AND NOTIONS
88 x 10 mm luster-finished beads
½ yd (50 cm) of coordinating heavy-weight furnishing fabric
Natural-colored rayon cord
16" (40 cm) diameter pillow form

NEEDLES
Size 10½ (7 mm)

GAUGE
11 sts x 13 rows = 4" (10 cm) in stockinette stitch using size 10½ (7 mm) needles

ABBREVIATIONS
k—knit; k1f&b—knit into front and back of stitch; p—purl; p1f&b—purl into front and back of stitch; RS—right side; st(s)—stitch(es); tbl—through back of loop; tog—together; WS—wrong side

FRONT

Using size 10½ (7 mm) needles, cast on 21 sts. Beginning at the bottom right of the chart on page 113, work the front, shaping the sides and placing purl stitches as indicated. Increase on RS rows by k1f&b; increase on WS rows by p1f&b. Decrease at the beginning of a row by k2tog tbl on RS rows and p2tog tbl on WS rows. Decrease at the end of a row by k2tog on RS rows and p2tog on WS rows. When the last row of the chart has been completed, bind off knitwise.

Knitting with suede thong is hard on the fingers, but well worth the effort. Choose large beads that will stand out from the texture of the suede.

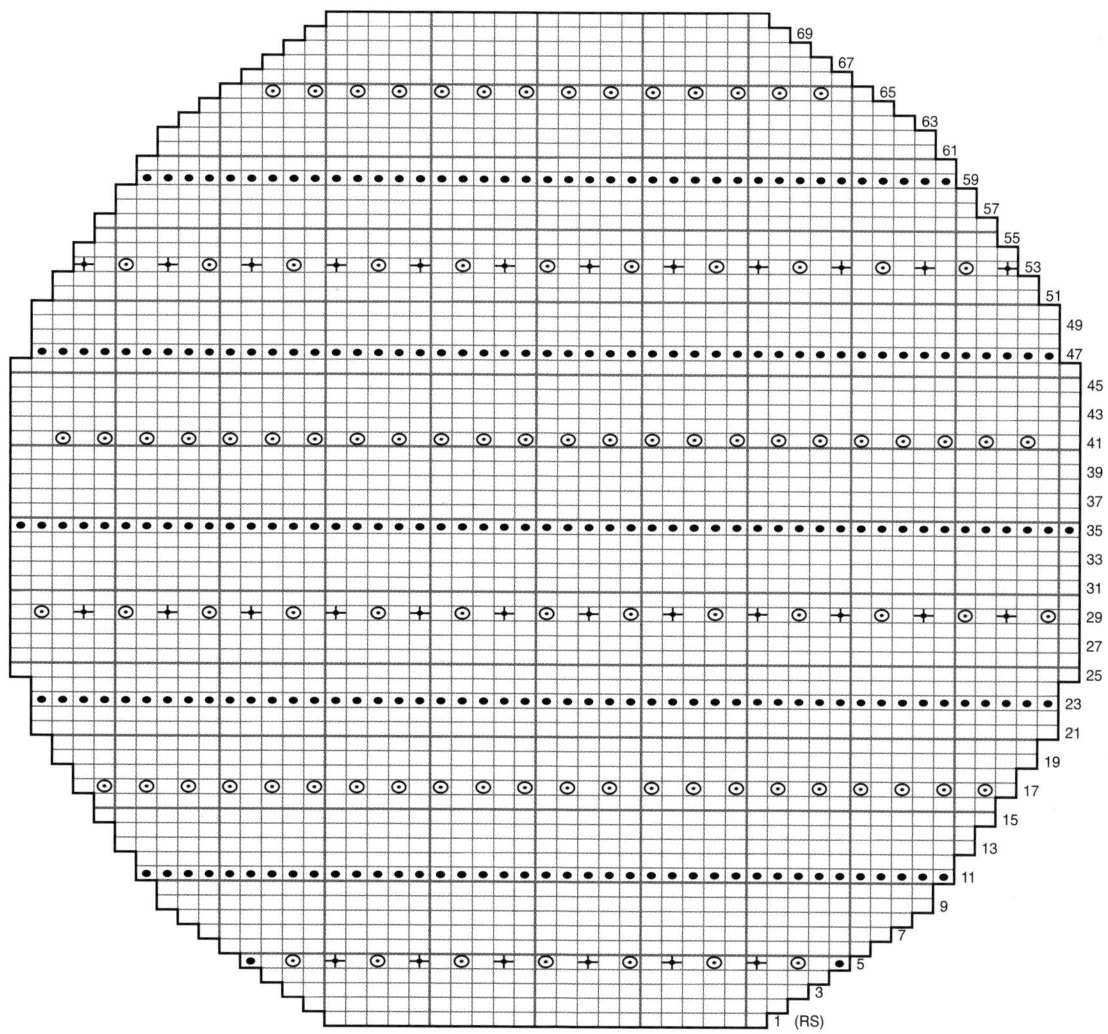

FINISHING

Weave in any loose ends. Sew beads in position as indicated on the chart using a doubled end of rayon cord, then attach tassels where indicated. Each tassel should be made from two 5½" (14 cm) lengths of suede thong and attached to the pillow using the same technique as for attaching a tassel fringe. Using the knitted piece as a template, cut a circle of fabric to line the pillow front, adding 1" (2.5 cm) all around as a seam allowance. Cut two pieces of fabric for the pillow back, allowing a 1" (2.5 cm) seam allowance all the way around the curved edges plus a 2½" (6 cm) overlap at the straight center edge. Turn a ⅝" (15 mm) deep hem along each straight center edge of the back fabric pieces and sew using a sewing machine. With RS together, place the fabric back onto the fabric front, taking care to overlap the back pieces, and sew together. Turn the fabric cover RS out and overcast the knitted piece onto the front using suede thong. Using rayon cord, make four loop fastenings evenly spaced along the top edge of the back opening, making sure that they are large enough to pass a bead through. Sew beads in place on the other back piece to match the positions of the loops. Insert the pillow form and fasten the buttons.

KEY

- k on RS, p on WS
- p on RS, k on WS
- k on RS, then sew bead to st during finishing
- k on RS, then attach tassel to st during finishing

New skills

Tassel fringe, see page 96
Loop fastenings, see page 58

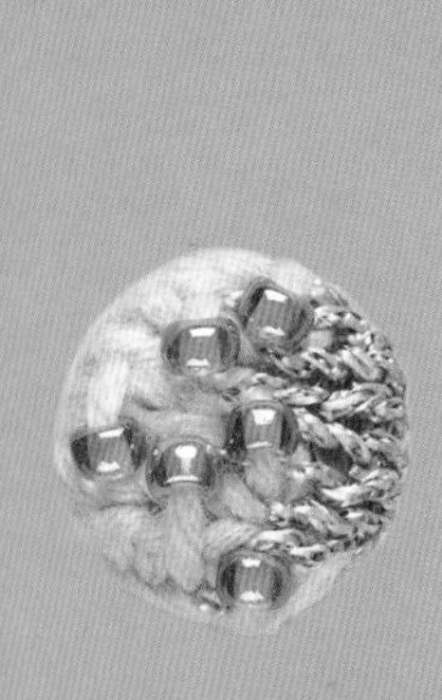

Quick & easy embellishments

This section has lots of designs that can be used to finish off both beaded and unbeaded projects, including buttons, corsages, and trims. Whatever your skill level, all of these embellishments can be completed quickly, and once you have worked them in the yarns and beads or sequins specified here, you can experiment with different materials and needle sizes for a wider variety of looks. Most of the trims are knitted lengthwise, which means you can measure as you work to ensure that you make the right length of trim for the project you are edging. For those that are knitted widthwise, knit a small test piece to calculate how many stitches you will need to cast on to fit the project you wish to trim.

Experiment and enjoy!

BUTTONS

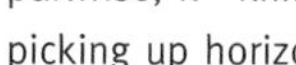

Denim button

Measurements
5/8" (1.5 cm) diameter

Yarn
Scrap of DK-weight yarn (100% cotton denim; approx. 102 yds/93 m per 2 oz/50 g ball) in blue

Beads
8 x 3 mm green beads

Needles
Size 3 (3.25 mm)

Gauge
23 sts x 35 rows = 4" (10 cm) in stockinette stitch using size 3 (3.25 mm) needles before washing; 23 sts x 40 rows = 4" (10 cm) after washing

Abbreviations
bead 1—place 1 bead and slip 1 stitch purlwise; k—knit; m1—make 1 stitch by picking up horizontal bar before next stitch and knitting into back of it; p—purl; RS—right side; st(s)—stitch(es); tog—together

KNITTING THE BUTTON

Thread the beads onto the yarn. Using size 3 (3.25 mm) needles, cast on 5 sts.
Row 1 (RS): K1, (bead 1, k1) twice.
Row 2: P1, m1, purl to last st, m1, p1 (7 sts).
Row 3: K2, (bead 1, k1) twice, k1.
Row 4: Purl.
Rows 5–7: Repeat rows 3–4 once, then row 3 again.
Row 8: P2tog, purl to last 2 sts, p2tog (5 sts).
Bind off knitwise, leaving a long end of yarn.

FINISHING

Thread a needle with the long end of yarn (weave in any other loose ends first). With WS together, fold the edges toward the center. Run the yarn through the edge stitches and pull up as tightly as possible to make a button shape, using a small amount of spare yarn as a filling to help form the shape. Fasten off, leaving another long end of yarn to sew the button in place.

Two-tone button

Measurements
5/8" (1.5 cm) diameter

Yarn
A Scrap of light-weight yarn (80% viscose, 20% polyester; approx. 103 yds/95 m per 1 oz/25 g ball) in metallic pink
B Scrap of DK-weight yarn (75% cotton, 25% microfiber; approx. 175 yds/160 m per 2 oz/50 g ball) in pink

Beads
6 x 3 mm pink beads

Needles
Size 7 (4.5 mm)

Gauge
22 sts x 30 rows = 4" (10 cm) in stockinette stitch using size 7 (4.5mm) needles

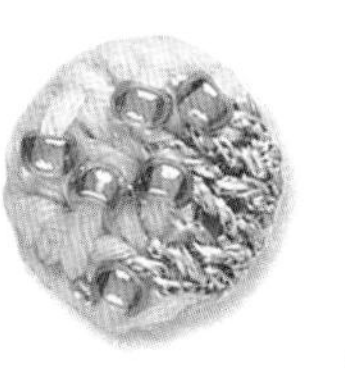

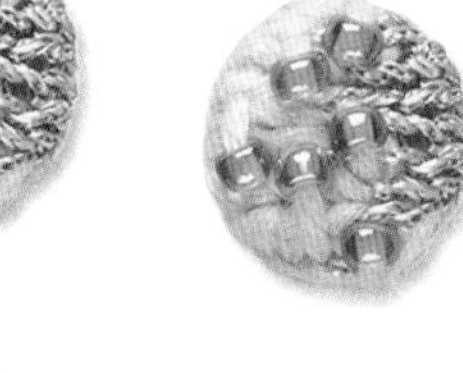

Abbreviations
bead 1—place 1 bead and slip 1 stitch purlwise; k—knit; m1—make 1 stitch by picking up horizontal bar before next stitch and knitting into back of it; RS—right side; st(s)—stitch(es); tog—together

KNITTING THE BUTTON

Thread the beads onto yarn B. Using size 7 (4.5 mm) needles and yarn A, cast on 5 sts.
Row 1 (RS): Knit.
Row 2: Purl.
Row 3: K1, m1, knit to last st, m1, k1 (7 sts).
Row 4: Purl.
Rows 5–6: Repeat rows 3–4 (9 sts).
Break off yarn A and join yarn B.
Row 7: K2, (bead 1, k1) to last st, k1.
Row 8: Purl.
Row 9: K2tog, (k1, bead 1) twice, k1, k2tog (7 sts).
Row 10: Purl.
Row 11: K2tog, k1, bead 1, k1, k2tog (5 sts).
Row 12: Purl.
Bind off, leaving a long end of yarn.

FINISHING

Thread a needle with the long end of yarn (weave in any other loose ends first). With WS together, fold the edges toward the center. Run the yarn through the edge stitches and pull up as tightly as possible to make a button, using a small amount of spare yarn as a filling to help form the shape. Fasten off, leaving another long end of yarn to sew the button in place.

CORSAGES

Daytime corsage

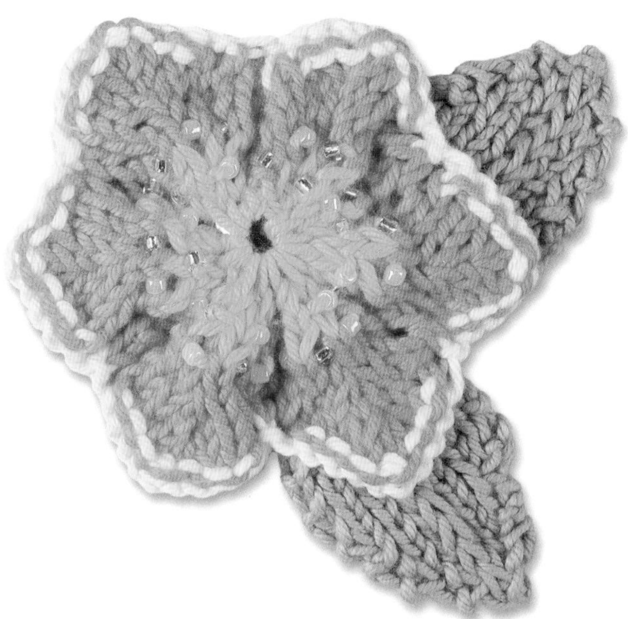

Measurements
Flower = 4" (10 cm) diameter

Yarn
Scraps of DK-weight yarn (100% cotton; approx. 93 yds/85 m per 2 oz/50 g ball):
A Yellow
B Pink
C Orange
D Green

Beads and notions
15 x 3 mm white beads
15 x 3 mm clear beads
1¼" (3 cm) long pin clip

Needles
Size 7 (4.5 mm)

Gauge
20 sts x 28 rows = 4" (10 cm) in stockinette stitch using size 7 (4.5 mm) needles

Abbreviations
bead 1—place 1 bead and slip 1 stitch purlwise; k—knit; p—purl; RS—right side; sl 1—slip 1 stitch knitwise; st(s)—stitch(es); tbl—through back of loop; tog—together; yo—yarn over

FLOWER
Thread the beads onto yarn C, alternating colors. Using size 7 (4.5 mm) needles and yarn A, cast on 61 sts. Break off yarn A and join yarn B.
Row 1 (RS): *K1, yo, p3, p3tog, p3, yo, repeat from * to last st, k1.
Row 2: Purl.
Row 3: *K1, yo, k3, k3tog, k3, yo, repeat from * to last st, k1.
Rows 4–5: Repeat rows 2–3.
Row 6: Purl.
Break off yarn B and join yarn C.
Row 7: (K1, bead 1) to last st, k1.
Row 8: P2tog to last st, p1 (31 sts).
Rows 9–10: Repeat rows 7–8 (16 sts).
Break off yarn and draw tightly through remaining 16 sts to fasten off.

LEAVES (make 2)
Using size 7 (4.5 mm) needles and yarn D, cast on 9 sts.
Row 1 (RS): K4, sl 1, k4.
Row 2: K1, purl to last st, k1.
Rows 3–6: Repeat rows 1–2 twice.
Row 7: K2tog tbl, k2, sl 1, k2, k2tog (7 sts).
Row 8: K1, purl to last st, k1.
Row 9: K3, sl 1, k3.
Row 10: K1, purl to last st, k1.
Row 11: K2tog tbl, k1, sl 1, k1, k2tog (5 sts).
Row 12: K1, purl to last st, k1.
Row 13: K2tog tbl, sl 1, k2tog (3 sts).
Row 14: P3tog and fasten off.

FINISHING
Weave in any loose ends. Fold the flower RS together and sew the side seam. Sew the leaves to the underside of the flower below adjacent petals. Sew a pin clip to the center back using sewing thread.

Evening corsage

Measurements
6" (15 cm) diameter at widest point

Yarn
Scraps of light-weight yarn (100% cotton; approx. 137 yds/115 m per 2 oz/50 g ball):
A Purple
B Red
C Brown

Beads and notions
Selection of decorative beads
1¼" (3 cm) long pin clip
8" (20 cm) length of 1" (2.5 cm) wide sheer ribbon

Needles
Size 3 (3.25 mm)

Gauge
23 sts x 32 rows = 4" (10 cm) in stockinette stitch using size 3 (3.25 mm) needles

Abbreviations
k—knit; m1—make 1 stitch by picking up horizontal bar before next stitch and

knitting into back of it; p—purl; RS—right side; st(s)—stitch(es); tbl—through back of loop; tog—together; WS—wrong side; yo—yarn over

BASE

Using size 3 (3.25 mm) needles and yarn C, cast on 4 sts.
Row 1 (RS): Knit.
Row 2: K1, m1, purl to last st, m1, k1 (6 sts).
Row 3: K1, m1, knit to last st, m1, k1 (8 sts).
Row 4: As row 2 (10 sts).
Row 5: Knit.
Row 6: As row 2 (12 sts).
Row 7: Knit.
Row 8: K1, purl to last st, k1.
Row 9: Knit.
Row 10: K1, purl to last st, k1.
Row 11: Knit.
Row 12: K2tog, purl to last 2 sts, k2tog (8 sts).
Row 13: K2tog, knit to last 2 sts, k2tog (6 sts).
Row 14: As row 12 (4 sts).
Bind off knitwise.

OUTER PETALS (make 4)

Using size 3 (3.25 mm) needles and yarn B, cast on 3 sts.
Row 1 (RS): Knit.
Row 2: K1, p1, k1.
Row 3: (K1, m1) twice, k1 (5 sts).
Row 4: K1, m1, p3, m1, k1 (7 sts).
Row 5: K1, m1, k1, k2tog, yo, k2, m1, k1 (9 sts).
Row 6: K1, m1, purl to last st, m1, k1 (11 sts).
Row 7: Knit.
Row 8: K1, purl to last st, k1.
Row 9: K4, k2tog, yo, knit to end.
Row 10: K1, purl to last st, k1.
Row 11: Knit.
Row 12: K1, purl to last st, k1.
Rows 13–16: Repeat rows 9–12.
Row 17: K4, k2tog, yo, knit to end.
Row 18: K2tog, purl to last 2 sts, k2tog (9 sts).
Row 19: Knit.
Row 20: K1, purl to last st, k1.
Row 21: K3, k2tog, yo, knit to end.
Row 22: K1, purl to last st, k1.
Row 23: K2, k2tog tbl, k1, k2tog, k2 (7 sts).
Row 24: K1, purl to last st, k1.
Row 25: K1, k2tog tbl, k1, k2tog, k1 (5 sts).
Row 26: K1, purl to last st, k1.
Row 27: K2tog tbl, k1, k2tog (3 sts).
Row 28: P3tog.
Fasten off yarn.

INNER PETALS (make 4)

Using size 3 (3.25 mm) needles and yarn A, cast on 10 sts.
Row 1 (RS): Knit.
Row 2: K1, purl to last st, k1.
Row 3: K1, m1, knit to last 2 sts, k2tog.
Row 4: K2tog, purl to last st, m1, k1.
Row 5: K1, m1, (yo, k2tog) to last 3 sts, yo, k1, k2tog (11 sts).
Row 6: K1, purl to last st, k1.
Row 7: K2tog, knit to last st, m1, k1.
Row 8: K1, m1, purl to last 2 sts, k2tog.
Row 9: K2tog, knit to last st, m1, k1.
Row 10: K1, purl to last st, k1.
Bind off knitwise.

FINISHING

Weave in any loose ends, then block and steam gently. Arrange the four outer petals evenly on the base and sew in place. Sew an inner petal between each pair of outer petals so that base is completely covered. Sew loops of sheer ribbon between pairs of inner petals to create another layer of petals. Decorate the center of the corsage with beaded tassels, attaching them like you would a tassel fringe (see page 96). Sew a pin clip to the center back using sewing thread.

LACE TRIMS

1: Two-color beaded trim

Measurements
This trim is knitted lengthwise and measures 1½" (4 cm) wide

Yarn
Light-weight yarn (100% cotton; approx. 137 yds/115 m per 2 oz/50 g ball) in pink

Beads
3 mm white beads
3 mm pink beads

Needles
Size 3 (3.25 mm)

Gauge
23 sts x 32 rows = 4" (10 cm) in stockinette stitch using size 3 (3.25 mm) needles

Abbreviations
bead 1—place 1 bead and slip 1 stitch purlwise; k—knit; RS—right side; sl 1—slip 1 stitch knitwise; st(s)—stitch(es); tog—together; WS—wrong side; yo—yarn over

KNITTING THE TRIM

Thread the beads onto the yarn, alternating four beads of each color. Using size 3 (3.25 mm) needles, cast on 9 sts.
Row 1 (RS): K2, bead 1, k1, sl 1, k1, bead 1, k2.
Row 2: K1, purl to last st, k1.
Rows 3–8: Repeat rows 1–2 three times.
Row 9: K1, k2tog, yo, k1, sl 1, k1, yo, k2tog, k1.
Row 10: K1, purl to last st, k1.
Rows 11–16: Repeat rows 9–10 three times.
Repeat rows 1–16 until trim is the desired length.

NOTE: Yarn quantities for trims
The size of project you are edging will dictate the quantity of yarn you will require. Measure how long the trim is after you have finished the first ball of yarn to check how many balls you will need to edge the project. The sooner you start the trim after having bought the yarn, the more likely it will be that you can purchase more yarn from that dye lot if you need to. Always err on the generous side when buying yarn to try to avoid this problem.

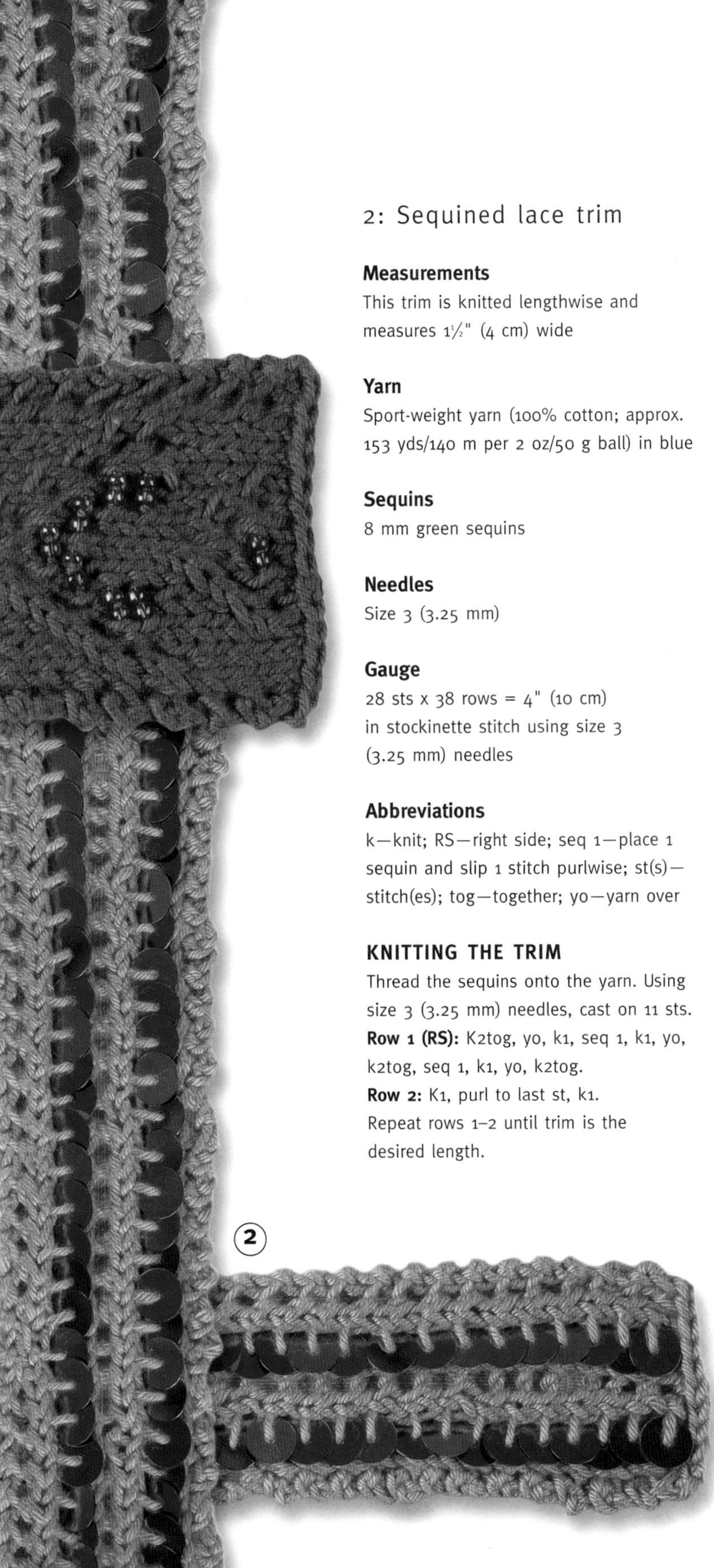

2: Sequined lace trim

Measurements
This trim is knitted lengthwise and measures 1½" (4 cm) wide

Yarn
Sport-weight yarn (100% cotton; approx. 153 yds/140 m per 2 oz/50 g ball) in blue

Sequins
8 mm green sequins

Needles
Size 3 (3.25 mm)

Gauge
28 sts x 38 rows = 4" (10 cm) in stockinette stitch using size 3 (3.25 mm) needles

Abbreviations
k—knit; RS—right side; seq 1—place 1 sequin and slip 1 stitch purlwise; st(s)—stitch(es); tog—together; yo—yarn over

KNITTING THE TRIM

Thread the sequins onto the yarn. Using size 3 (3.25 mm) needles, cast on 11 sts.
Row 1 (RS): K2tog, yo, k1, seq 1, k1, yo, k2tog, seq 1, k1, yo, k2tog.
Row 2: K1, purl to last st, k1.
Repeat rows 1–2 until trim is the desired length.

3: Beaded chevron trim

Measurements
This trim is knitted lengthwise and measures 3" (7.5 cm) wide

Yarn
DK-weight yarn (100% cotton; approx. 93 yds/85 m per 2 oz/50 g ball) in purple

Beads
3 mm red beads

Needles
Size 6 (4 mm)

Gauge
20 sts x 28 rows = 4" (10 cm) in stockinette stitch using size 6 (4 mm) needles

Abbreviations
bead 1—place 1 bead and slip 1 stitch purlwise; k—knit; p—purl; RS—right side; st(s)—stitch(es); tog—together; WS—wrong side; yo—yarn over

KNITTING THE TRIM

Thread the beads onto the yarn. Using size 6 (4 mm) needles, cast on 15 sts.
Row 1 (RS): K2tog, yo, k4, k2tog, yo, k5, yo, k2tog.
Row 2 & all unspecified WS rows: K1, purl to last st, k1.
Row 3: K2tog, yo, k3, k2tog, yo, k1, yo, k2tog, k3, yo, k2tog.
Row 5: K2tog, yo, k2, k2tog, yo, k1, bead 1, k1, yo, k2tog, k2, yo, k2tog.
Row 7: K2tog, yo, k1, k2tog, yo, k1, (bead 1, k1) twice, yo, k2tog, k1, yo, k2tog.
Row 9: (K2tog, yo) twice, k1, bead 1, k3, bead 1, k1, (yo, k2tog) twice.
Row 11: As row 9.
Row 12: K1, purl to last st, k1.
Repeat rows 1–12 until trim is the desired length.

FRINGED TRIMS

1: Beaded bell edging

Measurements
This trim is knitted widthwise and measures 1⅝" (4 cm) wide

Yarn
DK-weight yarn (70% alpaca, 30% silk; approx. 289 yds/265 m per 4 oz/100 g ball) in honey

Beads
3 mm gold beads

Needles
Size 6 (4 mm)

Gauge
22 sts x 30 rows = 4" (10 cm) in stockinette stitch using size 6 (4 mm) needles

Abbreviations
bead 1—place 1 bead and slip 1 stitch purlwise; k—knit; p—purl; psso—pass slip stitch over; RS—right side; sl 1—slip 1 stitch knitwise; skpo—slip 1, knit 1, pass slip stitch over; st(s)—stitch(es); tog—together; WS—wrong side; yb—take yarn between needles to back

KNITTING THE TRIM

Thread the beads onto the yarn. Using size 6 (4 mm) needles, cast on a multiple of 12 sts plus 3 sts, depending on how long you want the trim to be.

Row 1 (RS): P3, *(k1, bead 1) 4 times, k1, p3, repeat from * to end.
Row 2: K3, *p9, k3, repeat from * to end.
Row 3 (decrease row): P3, *yb, skpo, k5, k2tog, p3, repeat from * to end.
Row 4: K3, *p7, k3, repeat from * to end.
Row 5 (decrease row): P3, *yb, skpo, k3, k2tog, p3, repeat from * to end.
Row 6: K3, *p5, k3, repeat from * to end.
Row 7 (decrease row): P3, *yb, skpo, k1, k2tog, p3, repeat from * to end.
Row 8: K3, *p3, k3, repeat from * to end.
Row 9 (decrease row): P3, *yb, sl 1, k2tog, psso, p3, repeat from * to end.
Row 10: K3, *p1, k3, repeat from * to end.
Row 11 (decrease row): P3, *bead 1, p3, repeat from * to end.
Row 12: K3, *p1, k3, repeat from * to end.
Rows 13–14: Repeat rows 11–12 once.
Bind off in pattern.

2: Beaded loopy fringe

Measurements
This trim is knitted lengthwise and measures 1⅛" (3 cm) wide excluding fringe

Yarn
DK-weight yarn (57% merino wool, 33% microfiber, 10% cashmere; approx. 142 yds/130 m per 2 oz/50 g ball) in orange

Beads
3 mm red beads

Needles
Size 6 (4 mm)

Gauge
22 sts x 30 rows = 4" (10 cm) in stockinette stitch using size 6 (4 mm) needles

Abbreviations
bead 1—place 1 bead and slip 1 stitch purlwise; k—knit; ML—make $1\frac{5}{8}$" (4 cm) long loop (see page 33); RS—right side; st(s)—stitch(es)

KNITTING THE TRIM

Thread the beads onto the yarn. Using size 6 (4 mm) needles, cast on 7 sts.

Row 1 (RS): K1, (ML, k1) twice, bead 1, k1.
Row 2: K1, purl to last st, k1.
Row 3: K2, ML, k2, bead 1, k1.
Row 4: K1, purl to last st, k1.
Repeat rows 1–4 until trim is desired length.

3: Sequined cobweb trim

Measurements
This trim is knitted widthwise and measures $1\frac{3}{8}$" (3.5 cm) wide

Yarn
Light-weight yarn (100% cotton; approx. 137 yds/115 m per 2 oz/50 g ball) in red

Sequins
8 mm gold sequins

Needles
Size 3 (3.25 mm)

Gauge
23 sts x 32 rows = 4" (10 cm) in stockinette stitch using size 3 (3.25 mm) needles

Abbreviations
k—knit; p—purl; RS—right side; seq 1—place 1 sequin and slip 1 stitch purlwise; st(s)—stitch(es); tbl—through back of loop; WS—wrong side

KNITTING THE TRIM

Thread the sequins onto the yarn. Using size 3 (3.25 mm) needles, cast on a multiple of 3 sts plus 1 st, depending on how long you want the trim to be.

Row 1 (WS): (P1, seq 1) to last st, p1.
Row 2 (RS): K1 tbl, *p2, k1 tbl, repeat from * to end.
Row 3: P1, *k1 tbl, k1, p1, repeat from * to end.
Row 4: As row 2.
Rows 5–8: Repeat rows 3–4 twice.
Row 9: P1, *k1 tbl, slip next st off needle and allow it to drop down to cast-on edge, p1, repeat from * to end.
Row 10: K1 tbl, *p1, k1 tbl, repeat from * to end.
Row 11: P1, *k1 tbl, p1, repeat from * to end.
Bind off in pattern.

SHAPED TRIMS

1: Pearly pointed trim

Measurements
This trim is knitted lengthwise and measures 2½" (6.5 cm) wide

Yarn
DK-weight yarn (75% cotton, 25% microfiber; approx. 175 yds/160 m per 2 oz/50 g ball) in pink

Sequins
8 mm clear sequins
8 mm pearl sequins

Needles
Size 6 (4 mm)

Gauge
22 sts x 30 rows = 4" (10 cm) in stockinette stitch using size 6 (4 mm) needles

Abbreviations
k1f&b—knit into front and back of stitch; RS—right side; seq 1—place 1 sequin and slip 1 stitch purlwise; st(s)—stitch(es)

KNITTING THE TRIM
Thread the sequins onto the yarn, alternating the colors. Using size 6 (4 mm) needles, cast on 7 sts.
Row 1 (RS): K1f&b, seq 1, knit to end (8 sts).
Row 2: Knit to last st, k1f&b (9 sts).
Rows 3–8: Repeat rows 1–2 three times (15 sts).
Row 9: K1, seq 1, knit to end.
Row 10: knit.
Row 11: Bind off 8 sts knitwise, knit to end (7 sts).
Row 12: Knit.
Repeat rows 1–12 until trim is the desired length.

2: Two-tone castle trim

Measurements
This trim is knitted lengthwise and measures 2" (5 cm) wide

Yarn
Light-weight yarn (100% cotton; approx. 137 yds/115 m per 2 oz/50 g ball):
A Lime
B Green

Beads
3 mm blue beads
3 mm yellow beads
Quantities of each should be divisible by 5

Needles
Size 3 (3.25 mm)

Gauge
23 sts x 32 rows = 4" (10 cm) in stockinette stitch using size 3 (3.25 mm) needles

Abbreviations
bead 1—place 1 bead and slip 1 stitch purlwise; k—knit; m1—make 1 stitch by picking up horizontal bar before next stitch and knitting into back of it; RS—right side; st(s)—stitch(es); tbl—through back of loop; tog—together

KNITTING THE TRIM
Thread the yellow beads onto yarn A and the blue beads onto yarn B. Using size 3 (3.25 mm) needles and yarn A, cast on 10 sts.
Row 1 (RS): Knit.
Row 2: K1, purl to last 2 sts, m1, k2 (11 sts).
Row 3: K2, m1, knit to end (12 sts).
Row 4: As row 2 (13 sts).
Row 5: K3, (bead 1, k1) to end.
Row 6: K1, purl to last 2 sts, k2.
Row 7: K1, k2tog tbl, knit to end (12 sts).
Row 8: K1, purl to last 3 sts, k2tog, k1 (11 sts).
Row 9: K1, k2tog tbl, knit to end (10 sts).
Rows 10–12: Knit.
Break off yarn A and join yarn B.

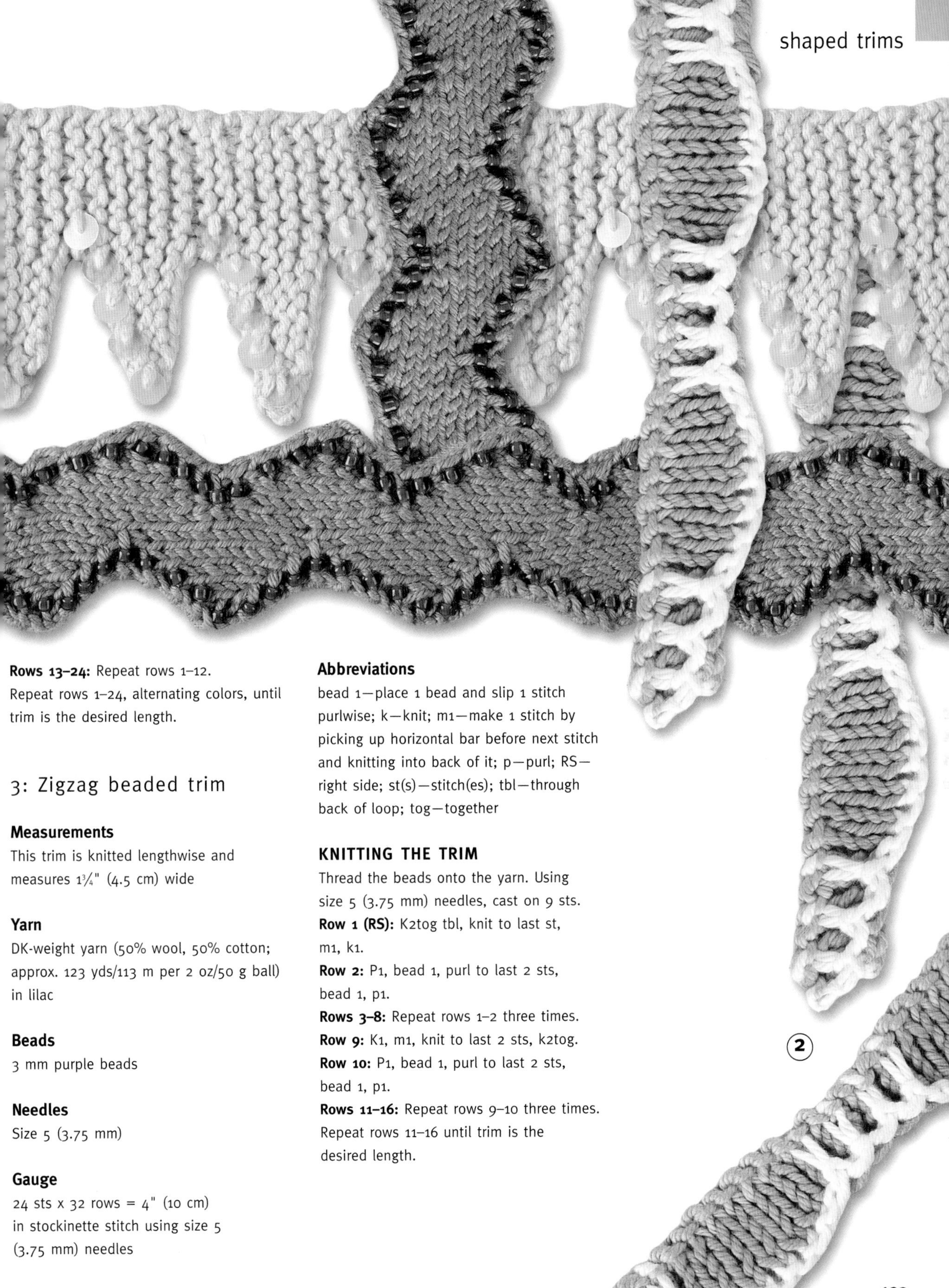

Rows 13–24: Repeat rows 1–12.
Repeat rows 1–24, alternating colors, until trim is the desired length.

3: Zigzag beaded trim

Measurements
This trim is knitted lengthwise and measures 1¾" (4.5 cm) wide

Yarn
DK-weight yarn (50% wool, 50% cotton; approx. 123 yds/113 m per 2 oz/50 g ball) in lilac

Beads
3 mm purple beads

Needles
Size 5 (3.75 mm)

Gauge
24 sts x 32 rows = 4" (10 cm) in stockinette stitch using size 5 (3.75 mm) needles

Abbreviations
bead 1—place 1 bead and slip 1 stitch purlwise; k—knit; m1—make 1 stitch by picking up horizontal bar before next stitch and knitting into back of it; p—purl; RS—right side; st(s)—stitch(es); tbl—through back of loop; tog—together

KNITTING THE TRIM

Thread the beads onto the yarn. Using size 5 (3.75 mm) needles, cast on 9 sts.
Row 1 (RS): K2tog tbl, knit to last st, m1, k1.
Row 2: P1, bead 1, purl to last 2 sts, bead 1, p1.
Rows 3–8: Repeat rows 1–2 three times.
Row 9: K1, m1, knit to last 2 sts, k2tog.
Row 10: P1, bead 1, purl to last 2 sts, bead 1, p1.
Rows 11–16: Repeat rows 9–10 three times.
Repeat rows 11–16 until trim is the desired length.

Yarn directory

Below is a list of the specific yarns used to make the projects. If you cannot find any of these yarns or simply wish to make an accessory in a different yarn, use the information supplied here to help you choose a suitable alternative. Refer also to the beginning of each project, where you will find the quantity, weight, and fiber content of the yarns used to make each project.

Project 1: FUNKY FELTED BELT
Yarn: Rowan Yorkshire Tweed DK; colors & codes: A = Scarlet 344, B = Frolic 350; needles: size 6 (4 mm); gauge: 20–22 sts x 28–30 rows.

Project 2: SLANTED SEQUINED SCARF
Yarn: RYC Cashsoft DK; colors & codes: A = Cream 500, B = Clementine 501, C = Bloom 520, D = Poison 513, E = Madam 511; needles: size 6 (4 mm); gauge: 22 sts x 30 rows.

Project 3: LACED BIKINI
Yarn: Rowan Cotton Glace; color & code: In The Pink 189; needles: size 3–5 (3.25–3.5 mm); gauge: 23 sts x 32 rows.

NOTE: Needle size and gauge
The needle size and gauge supplied here are those recommended on the ball band of the yarn. Note that they are NOT the needle size and gauge that you should use to make the projects. Sometimes a project pattern specifies a different needle size and gauge from those recommended by the manufacturer in order to achieve a certain look. The information supplied here is simply to help you select a substitute yarn, if you wish to do so, that matches the weight of the original yarn as closely as possible so that you can achieve comparable results in the finished project.

Project 4: BEADED FLOAT CHOKER AND BRACELET
Yarn: Jaeger Siena (4ply); color & code: Borage 424; needles: size 2–3 (2.5–3 mm); gauge: 28 sts x 38 rows.

Project 5: SNUGGLY COLLAR AND CUFFS
Yarn A: Rowan Calmer; color & code: Blush 477; needles: size 8 (5 mm); gauge: 21 sts x 30 rows. Yarn B: Rowan Kidsilk Haze; color & code: Splendour 579; needles: size 3–8 (3.25–5 mm); gauge: 18–25 sts x 23–34 rows.

Project 6: BUCKLED SATCHEL
Yarn A: Rowan Summer Tweed; color & code: Summer Berry 537; needles: size 8 (5 mm); gauge 16 sts x 23 rows. Yarn B: Rowan Wool Cotton; color & code: Pumpkin 962; needles: size 5–6 (3.75–4 mm); gauge: 22–24 sts x 30–32 rows.

Project 7: SLOUCHY SUMMER BAG
Yarn: Rowan Cotton Rope; color & code: Squash 061; needles: size 10 (6 mm); gauge: 15 sts x 20 rows.

Project 8: SEQUINED FLAPPER BAG
Yarn: Rowan Cotton Glace; color & code: Blood Orange 445; needles: size 3–5 (3.25–3.5 mm); gauge: 23 sts x 32 rows.

Project 9: FELTED BAG AND CHANGE PURSE
Yarn: Rowan Yorkshire Tweed DK; colors & codes: A = Skip 347, B = Frolic 350, C = Goose 352, D = Frog 349, E = Rowdy 35; needles: size 6 (4 mm); gauge: 20–22 sts x 28–30 rows.

Project 10: DOTTY DENIM BAG
Yarn: Rowan Denim; color & code: Tennessee 231; needles: size 6 (4 mm); gauge: 20 sts x 28 rows before washing; 20 sts x 32 rows after washing.

Project 11: BEADED FLOAT SKIRT
Yarn: Rowan Denim; color & code: Memphis 229; needles: size 6 (4 mm); gauge: 20 sts x 28 rows before washing; 20 sts x 32 rows after washing.

Project 12: SUMPTUOUSLY SOFT SHRUG
Yarn: UK Alpaca; color: Honey; needles: size 4–6 (3.5–4 mm); gauge: 22 sts x 30 rows.

Project 13: SEQUINED COLLAR CAPE
Yarn: RYC Soft Tweed; color & code: Antique 002; needles: size 11 (8 mm); gauge: 12 sts x 16 rows.

Project 14: LACY HIP-TIE V-NECK
Yarn A: Rowan Summer Tweed; color & code: Spring 527; needles: size 8 (5 mm); gauge: 16 sts x 23 rows. Yarn B: Rowan Cotton Glace; color & code: Shoot 814; needles: size 3–5 (3.25–3.5 mm); gauge: 23 sts x 32 rows.

Project 15: LUXURIOUS BEADED WRAP
Yarn: RYC Cashsoft 4ply; color & code: Loganberry 430; needles: size 3 (3.25 mm); gauge 28 sts x 36 rows.

Project 16: OPTIC-STRIPED PILLOW
Yarn: Rowan Wool Cotton; colors & codes: A = Violet 933, B = August 953, C = Antique 900, D = Small 963; needles: size 5–6 (3.75–4 mm); gauge: 22–24 sts x 30–32 rows.

Project 17: FLORAL STRIPED BOLSTER
Yarns A & B: Rowan Calmer; colors & codes: A = Powder Puff 482, B = Calmer 463; needles: size 8 (5 mm); gauge: 21 sts x 30 rows. Yarns C & D: Rowan Lurex Shimmer; colors & codes: C = Gleam 336, D = Pewter 333; needles: size 3 (3.25 mm); gauge: 29 sts x 41 rows.

Project 18: FLORAL SUMMER THROW
Yarn: Rowan Handknit Cotton; colors & codes: A = Mango Fool 319, B = Slick 313, C = Flame 254, D = Ecru 251, E = Decadent 314, F = Buttercup 320, G = Gooseberry 219, H = Seafarer 318; needles: size 6–7 (4–4.5 mm); gauge: 19–20 sts x 28 rows.

Project 19: JEWELED SCENTED SACHETS
Yarn: Rowan Cotton Glace; colors & codes: A = Tickle 811, B = Zeal 813, C = Blood Orange 445, D = Dijon 739; needles: size 3–5 (3.25–3.5 mm); gauge: 23 sts x 32 rows.

BUTTONS

Denim button
Yarn: Rowan Denim; color & code: Tennessee 231; needles: size 6 (4 mm); gauge: 20 sts x 28 rows before washing; 20 sts x 32 rows after washing.

Two-tone button
Yarn A: Rowan Lurex Shimmer; color & code: Gleam 336; needles: size 3 (3.25 mm); gauge: 29 sts x 41 rows.
Yarn B: Rowan Calmer; color & code: Powder Puff 482; needles: size 8 (5 mm); gauge: 21 sts x 30 rows.

CORSAGES

Daytime corsage
Yarn: Rowan Handknit Cotton; colors & codes: A = Buttercup 320, B = Slick 313, C = Mango Fool 319, D = Gooseberry 219; needles: size 6–7 (4–4.5 mm); gauge: 19–20 sts x 28 rows.

Evening corsage
Yarn: Rowan Cotton Glace; colors & codes: A = Excite 815, B = Blood Orange 445, C = Mocha Choc 816; needles: size 3–5 (3.25–3.5 mm); gauge: 23 sts x 32 rows.

LACE TRIMS

1: Two-color beaded trim
Yarn: Rowan Cotton Glace; color & code: Tickle 811; needles: size 3–5 (3.25–3.5 mm); gauge: 23 sts x 32 rows.

2: Sequined lace trim
Yarn: Jaeger Siena (4ply); color & code: Borage 424; needles: size 2–3 (2.5–3 mm); gauge: 28 sts x 38 rows.

3: Beaded chevron trim
Yarn: Rowan Handknit Cotton; color & code: Decadent 314; needles: size 6–7 (4–4.5 mm); gauge: 19–20 sts x 28 rows.

FRINGED TRIMS

1: Beaded bell edging
Yarn: UK Alpaca; color: Honey; needles: size 4–6 (3.5–4 mm); gauge: 22 sts x 30 rows.

2: Beaded loopy fringe
Yarn: RYC Cashsoft DK; color & code: Clementine 510; needles: size 6 (4 mm); gauge: 22 sts x 30 rows.

3: Sequined cobweb trim
Yarn: Rowan Cotton Glace; color & code: Blood Orange 445; needles: size 3–5 (3.25–3.5 mm); gauge: 23 sts x 32 rows.

SHAPED TRIMS

1: Pearly pointed trim
Yarn: Rowan Calmer; color & code: Powder Puff 482; needles: size 8 (5 mm); gauge: 21 sts x 30 rows.

2: Two-tone castle trim
Yarn: Rowan Cotton Glace; colors & codes: A = Zeal 813, B = Shoot 814; needles: size 3–5 (3.25–3.5 mm); gauge: 23 sts x 32 rows.

3: Zigzag beaded trim
Yarn: Rowan Wool Cotton; color & code: Violet 933; needles: size 5–6 (3.75–4 mm); gauge: 22–24 sts x 30–32 rows.

Resources

The yarns, beads, sequins, and other materials used in this book are available from good department stores and via mail-order and internet suppliers. Below is a selection of retail stores and web resources.

YARNS

A Back Door Bead and Yarn Co.
Tucson, AZ 85712
520-745-9080

Acorn Street Yarn Shop
Seattle, WA 98105
206-525-1726

A Knitted Peace
Littleton, CO 80120
303-730-0366

Aloha Yarn
Kaneohe, HI 96744
808-234-5865

Alphabet Soup
Madison, WI 53705
608-238-1329

Angel Hair Yarn Co.
Nashville, TN 37215
615-269-8833

Arcadia Knitting
Chicago, IL 60640
773-293-1211

Ben Franklin Crafts
Mitchell, SD 57301
605-996-5464

City Knits
Detroit, MI 48202
313-872-9665

Craft Corner
Woonsocket, RI 02895
401-762-3233

Creative Corner
W. Des Moines, IA 50265
515-255-7262

Downtown Yarns
New York, NY 10009
212-995-5991

Elegant Stitches
Miami, FL 33176
305-232-4005

Heidi's Yarnhaus
Mobile, AL 36609
251-342-0088

In Sheep's Clothing
Laramie, WY 82070
307-755-9276

In Stitches
Augusta, GA 30907
706-868-9276

Keep Me in Stitches!
Frederick, MD 21701
240-379-7740

Knit 'n Needle
Whitefish, MT 59937
406-862-6390

Knit One Smock Too
Winston Salem, NC 27104
336-765-9099

Knitter's Dream
Harrisburg, PA 17112
717-599-7665

Knit Wits
Jackson, MS 39211
601-957-9098

Naked Sheep
Bennington, VT 05201
802-440-9653

Personal Threads
Omaha, NE 68114
402-391-7733

Sheep to Shore
Nantucket, MA 02554
508-228-0038

Stitch DC, Inc.
Washington, DC 20003
202-487-4337

Westminster Fibers
4 Townsend West, Unit 8
Nashua, NH 03063
603-886-5041

BEADS AND NOTIONS

Atlantic Gems
8609 Second Avenue
#103B Silver Spring, MD 20910
401-624-4332

Auntie's Beads
4113 West 83rd Street
Prairie Village, KS 66208
913-642-7092

Bead All About It
2441 NW 43rd Street, Suite 19
Thornebrook Village
Gainesville, FL 32606
352-375-8198

Bead Creative
5401 Sheridan Drive
Williamsville, NY 14221
716-626-4182

Beads and More
4150 Mission Boulevard, Suite 111
San Diego, CA 92109
858-483-4190

Beads Galore
2123 S. Priest, Suite 201
Tempe, AZ 85282
480-921-3949

Beadworks
149 Washington Street
Norwalk, CT 06854
203-852-9194

Creative Beads
6130 West Park
Houma, LA 70364
985-873-0743

Fabric Place Center
399 Boylston Street
Boston, MA 02116
617-262-3140

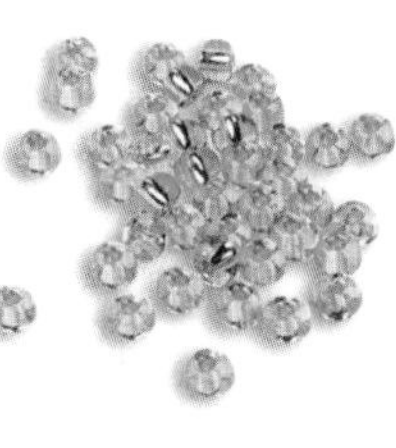

Fabric Place Center
Cowesett Corners
300 Quaker Lane
Warwick, RI 02886
401-823-5400

Haberman Fabrics
905 South Main Street
Royal Oak, MI 48067
248-541-0010

Knit One Bead Too
5269 Highway 12
Maple Plain, MN 55359
763-479-7125

Pacific Silverworks
461E Main Street, Suite A
Ventura, CA 93001
805-641-1394

Shipwreck Beads
8560 Commerce Place Drive NE
Dept B1 Lacey, WA 98516
800-950-4232

Wild About Beads
436 Main Road
Tiverton, RI 02878
401-624-4332

Worldly Treasures
1226 Washington Street
Mainitowoc, WI 54220
920-686-2323

WEB RESOURCES

Yarns
www.e-yarn.com
www.handworksgallery.com
www.hook-n-needle.com
www.kgctrading.com
www.knitrowan.com
www.knittersdream.com
www.knittingfever.com
www.lacis.com
www.mcadirect.com
www.patonsyarns.com
www.patternworks.com
www.personalthreads.com
www.sakonnetpurls.com
www.spiningayarn.com
www.theknittinggarden.com
www.yarncompany.com
www.yarnexpressions.com
www.yarnmarket.com

Beads and notions
www.auntiesbeads.com
www.beadexpo.com
www.beadingtimes.com
www.beadsgalore.com
www.beadwork.about.com
www.beadworks.com
www.beadwrangler.com
www.beadzunlimited.com
www.2beadornot2bead.com
www.7beads.com
www.ccartwright.com
www.craftsfaironline.com
www.fabricplace.com
www.habermanfabrics.com
www.guidetobeadwork.com
www.julesgems.com
www.knitonebeadtoo.net
www.members.cox.net/sdsantan/beadfairies.html
www.michaels.com
www.nationalbeadsociety.com
www.shipwreckbeads.com
www.pacificsilverworks.com

Index

AUTHOR'S ACKNOWLEDGMENTS
Thanks to Ann Hinchcliffe and all at Rowan/Jaeger/RYC for all their help and beautiful yarns. Kate Kirby and Michelle Pickering: well, we got there in the end. To my brilliant knitters Anthea McAlpin, Kathleen Dyne, Sue Hanmore, Jennifer Logan, and Carolyn Rattray: I really couldn't have done it without your help and nimble fingers. Sam Sloan: thanks as always for your support, patience, and brilliant photography (Snuggly Collar and Cuffs, project 5). Finally, I'd like to remember my amazing friend Julie Marchington: you're missed every day but never forgotten.